HEALTH CARE POLICY IN THE UNITED STATES

edited by
JOHN G. BRUHN
PENNSYLVANIA STATE
UNIVERSITY-HARRISBURG

A GARLAND SERIES

MEDICARE POLITICS

EXPLORING THE ROLES
OF MEDIA COVERAGE,
POLITICAL INFORMATION,
AND POLITICAL PARTICIPATION

Felicia E. Mebane

GARLAND PUBLISHING, INC.
A MEMBER OF THE TAYLOR & FRANCIS GROUP
NEW YORK & LONDON/2000

MT
HS

Published in 2000 by
Garland Publishing, Inc.
A member of the Taylor & Francis Group
29 West 35th Street
New York, NY 10001

10 9 8 7 6 5 4 3 2 1

Library of Congress Cataloging-in-Publication Data

Mebane, Felicia E.
    Medicare politics : exploring the media coverage, political
information, and political participation / Felicia e. Mebane.
        p.cm.-- (Health care policy in the United States)
    Includes bibliographical references and index.
    ISBN 0-8153-3717-5 (alk. paper)
        1. Medicare--Political aspects. 2. Medicare--Public opinion.
3. Public opinion--United States. I. Title. II. Series.

    RA412.3M42 2000
    368.4'26'00973--dc21
                                                    00-042232

Printed on acid-free, 250 year-life paper
Manufactured in the United States of America

11/21/01

To Mom and Dad

Contents

Introduction

Since 1965, Medicare has been an integral part of the political landscape in the United States. Medicare is the major source of health insurance for older Americans, who play a key role in electoral politics, is popular with the American public, and is a sizable portion of the federal budget. Thus, to understand major Medicare policy decisions, one must understand the politics surrounding the Medicare program.

This book includes three studies that further illuminate various aspects of a key political determinant of Medicare policy: public opinion. Chapter One examines media coverage of Medicare during the 1995 federal budget debates. Changes in the level of critical coverage of President Clinton and the Republican leadership are linked to changes in the public's support for their ability to address Medicare's problems. Additionally, the likelihood of critical coverage for various newsmakers during the debate is linked to topics covered during the debate to show which topics tended to have less critical coverage. Chapter Two uses public opinion data to explore whether or not knowledge of the Medicare program affected preferences for Medicare policy in 1995 during the last debate about major Medicare policy changes. Finally, participation in the election process is one manifestation of public opinion about campaign issues. In Chapter Three, political participation and mobilization of older and younger Americans in 1996, when Medicare was a campaign issue, is compared with corresponding rates of participation and mobilization in 1992 and 1988.

All three studies apply political science models and methods to a major public health program in order to provide insights into Medicare policy decisions. The final chapter translates lessons learned into implications for future Medicare policy debates.

Acknowledgments

I am thankful to many people for helping me to realize the goal of writing this dissertation. I thank Robert J. Blendon, my mentor, for inspiring me to pursue research topics that are fascinating, meaningful, and somewhat unique. I thank Keith Reeves, Penny Feldman, and Doug Staiger for contributing myriad perspectives on politics, health policy, and methods for analysis to the development of these studies.

I am also indebted to friends/colleagues, notably John Benson, Karen Donelan, Ted Brader, Kristina Hanson, Kathleen O'Neill, Nancy Beaulieu, Deborah Azrael, John T. Young, Pamela Berenbaum, Meredith Rosenthal, and David J. Cohen, who provided invaluable critiques and advice concerning numerous written and oral presentations of these ideas.

I am also thankful to everyone who provided me with data and financial support throughout the development of this manuscript. I thank Harvard University, the Agency for Health Care Policy and Research, Robert J. Blendon, Mollyann Brodie and the Henry J. Kaiser Family Foundation, and the Shorenstein Center at the Kennedy School of Government for providing these critical underpinnings for my research. I also thank Joan Curhan, Joe Newhouse, and other faculty and staff associated with the Ph.D. program in Health Policy for encouragement, advice, and guidance throughout the dissertation process.

Finally, I couldn't have earned this achievement without the love and support of family (Mom, Dad, Charlene, and Sheryl) and friends. Special thanks to the "family of friends" that I have developed within the Harvard community, especially my cohort (Amber Batata, Pam Berenbaum, Joanna Birckmayer, John Lavis, Meredith Rosenthal, and Jennifer Ruger), my Gov. 2000/2001 buddies, current and former members of Bob's group, Mollyann Brodie, and Haiden Huskamp.

List of Tables and Figures

TABLES

FIGURES

CHAPTER ONE

Media Coverage

The impending swell in the ranks of older Americans and rising medical costs ensure that Medicare will attain a prominent position on the national policy agenda in the near future. Once again, Congressional leaders, the President of the United States, and other policymakers will have to confront policy issues that could require fundamental changes to the Medicare program.

A crucial determinant of whether or not Medicare policy proposals become legislation is public support for the proposal.[1] As in previous Medicare policy debates, elected officials responsible for considering and implementing Medicare reform will use public opinion about reform proposals as support for their position or as a gauge of the likely political ramifications of their position.[2] The influence of public opinion on policymakers' decisions concerning changes to Medicare lead to the notion that factors influencing public opinion concerning Medicare are also important determinants of Medicare policy outcomes.

Media coverage is a key source of information about Medicare that affects public opinion and, indirectly, Medicare policy.[3] For the millions of Americans who watch or read stories about Medicare, media influence their opinions about proposals to reform Medicare and the ability of political leaders to address Medicare's problems by determining the information they receive about particular policy proposals and political leaders.[4] Thus, in order to understand public opinion concerning Medicare during upcoming policy debates, proponents of Medicare reform proposals should have an understanding of what information about Medicare media convey to the public.

Based on the predominant method used for analyzing the content of media coverage, this study presents statistics describing coverage of the Medicare debates in 1995-96 that can be used as a benchmark for patterns in future coverage. The analysis also provides evidence of how changes in one aspect of media coverage, criticism of newsmakers, correlate with shifts in public opinion concerning Medicare. The study ends with an examination of factors that explain variation in the level of criticism in coverage.

The first section below begins with a brief summary of the political environment and proposals that were the focus of media coverage during the last major debate about Medicare reform. Next is a discussion explaining the importance of opinion toward political leaders and describing the shifts in opinion that are later linked with changes in media coverage. The subsequent sections discuss how media affect public opinion and the focus of this study. A discussion of the data and methods used follows, along with descriptions of key variables. The final two sections present the results and a discussion of the implications.

SETTING THE STAGE

Debates concerning the composition of the federal budget in 1995 featured proposals to fundamentally change the Medicare program and occurred in an unusual political environment. The 1994 mid-term Congressional elections transformed the landscape of contemporary American politics and prominent political rhetoric. For the first time in 42 years, the Republican Party gained control of the House of Representatives. The accompanying Republican majority in the Senate, an increase in the percentage of Republican governors, and substantial increases in Republican State representatives lead many to herald the dawn of a new political era dominated by more conservative ideology (Stanley 1996).

Republicans' promises to lower taxes, create a balanced budget, and promote smaller, less intrusive government translated into efforts to restructure the Medicare program in a manner consistent with those goals.[5] House Speaker Newt Gingrich led efforts to craft a plan that would meet political goals and change the rate of spending for Medicare. The resulting proposal would have substantially altered Medicare.

For example, limits in payments to doctors and hospitals were accompanied by support for provider-sponsored networks to contract with the Medicare program. With regard to beneficiaries, various incentives were proposed to encourage Medicare beneficiaries to join lower cost health plans, such as health maintenance organizations (HMOs), or to establish medical savings accounts that would protect them from major medical costs. Additionally, most Medicare beneficiaries would have continued to pay the current level of monthly premiums for the portion of Medicare that pays for physician services (Part B), while the wealthiest beneficiaries would have been required to pay the entire cost of Part B coverage. The total package of proposed changes in the costs and benefits of Medicare would have affected the choices of every Medicare beneficiary and the payments of every Medicare provider.

As the minority party in both the House and Senate, Congressional Democrats had little influence on the content of the final Republican proposal. Their primary strategy throughout the debate was to resist Republicans' proposed changes to Medicare and to discredit Republican reforms by linking proposed savings from the program to a proposed tax cut.[6]

President Clinton countered Republicans' efforts with his own plan for addressing Medicare's financial issues. Although Clinton agreed with the need to slow the projected growth of Medicare, he rejected the size ($270 billion over seven years) and nature of the proposed GOP changes. As did the Republican plan, the White House plan relied primarily on reducing payments to providers to achieve its $124 billion of reductions in Medicare spending and expanded health care options for Medicare beneficiaries. In contrast to the Republican proposal, President Clinton proposed less substantial changes for beneficiaries and providers and rejected the idea of medical savings accounts and higher premiums for Part B. Finally, President Clinton's plan did not tie reductions in Medicare spending to efforts to meet federal budget targets. The White House plan also would have affected all Medicare beneficiaries and providers, but to a lesser extent than the Republican plan.

The first general measure of media coverage presented here shows the volume of Medicare coverage throughout the debate and discusses the activities that inspired changes in this measure (Figure 1). The April 3, 1995 Annual Report of the Medicare Board of Trustees sparked the beginning of a prolonged, heated political debate on Capitol Hill concerning the previously discussed proposals. The Trustee's report itself did not inspire a relatively high level of media coverage in April 1995. The total number of articles or stories about Medicare in March and April (26 and 20, respectively) were the lowest levels during the debate.

In contrast, political activity inspired by the content of the report generated a total of 155 articles or stories in May. Speeches and news conferences by Republican leadership focused the public's attention on the need to prevent Medicare's impending bankruptcy and on Republican plans to address this problem. Additionally, the 1995 White House Conference on Aging in early May provided a platform from which President Clinton responded to Republicans' proposals. Finally, by late May of 1995, the House and the Senate had debated and passed budget resolutions to reduce the Medicare budget by $256-282 billion. After May's run of articles and stories, the level of media coverage of Medicare never returned to the April low.

Figure 1: Amount of Media Coverage of Medicare (n=879)

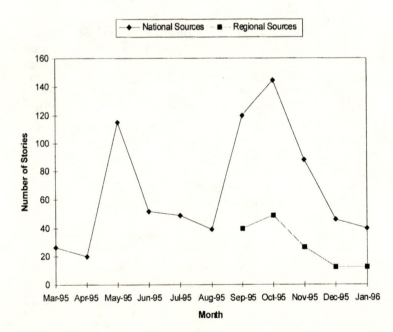

The highest levels of coverage occurred in September and October and were accompanied by the following political activity: By September 14th, an outline of the Republican legislative proposal began to circulate, and on September 29th, Republicans released a detailed plan for fundamental Medicare reform. The negotiations and debate escalated as the legislation moved through the Congress during October. The final bill was approved by Congress as part of a budget-reconciliation bill on November 17, 1995 and was vetoed by President Clinton on December 6, 1995. On December 9, 1995 President Clinton announced his own plans to revamp Medicare that were not formally considered by the Congress and faded into oblivion.

This brief account of the political and policy positions along with the volume of media coverage accompanying debate concerning Medicare sets the stage for subsequent analysis. The following section describes the public's support for the primary political actors during these debates.

PUBLIC OPINION TOWARDS POLITICAL LEADERS DEBATING MEDICARE REFORM

Efforts to reform Medicare in 1995-96 pitted Republicans against Democrats and President Clinton. At the same time, political leaders from each of these groups were battling to determine the size of the federal budget and deficit. Understanding the implications of significant changes to Medicare was an enterprise further complicated in 1995 by the need to factor into these analyses the likely impact on the federal deficit.

Because most Americans are not well-informed about the political system, I contend that general measures of the public's attitudes concerning political leaders spearheading Medicare reform efforts were a significant summary indicator of the public's attitudes about a range of aspects of Medicare reform, including the various policy options (Delli Carpini and Keeter 1996). Put differently, without specific knowledge about the politics of Medicare reform or the budget, the public's views about the political leaders are a major factor determining their support for Medicare reform efforts. Additionally, general measures of trust were often reported in media coverage as a straightforward way to frame the competition among political leaders for support of their reform efforts. Thus, this analysis focuses on changes in the public's confidence or trust in the ability of leaders of the two major political parties to deal with Medicare.[7]

When asked in June 1995 who would do a better job dealing with Medicare, one-third of Americans (33 percent) chose the Democratic Party, about one in five (22 percent) chose the Republican Party, and 37 percent chose both or neither political party (Table 1). After passage of the Republican budget proposal, a proportion of Americans who had not differentiated between the capabilities of the two parties in the previous survey supported the Democratic Party. In December 1995, 44 percent of Americans believed that the Democratic Party would do a better job dealing with Medicare and 26 percent chose both or neither party.

In a similar series of questions, Americans were asked whom they trusted to make decisions about Medicare (Table 2). Support for the Republican Party ranged from 32 percent in August 1995 to 39 percent in January 1996. The percentage of Americans who trusted President Bill Clinton to reform Medicare ranged from 47 percent in August 1995 to 58 percent in October 1995.

Table 1: Americans' Choice for Which Political Party Would Do a Better Job Dealing with Medicare

	% Who Favor 6/2/95	% Who Favor 12/1/95
Democratic Party	33	44
Republican Party	22	24
Both about the same	18	13
Neither	19	13
Not sure	8	6

Source: Data from NBC News/*Wall Street Journal* polls.

Table 2: Americans' Choice for Whom They Trust to Make Decisions About Medicare

	% Who Trust 8/23/95[1]	% Who Trust 10/27/95[2]	% Who Trust 1/2/96[3]
Republicans in Congress	32	34	39
Bill Clinton	47	58	50
Both (vol.)	—	1	1
Neither (vol.)	11	6	5
Don't know/No opinion or answer	10	2	5

[1] *Source*: Data from a *Time*/C.N.N./Yankelovich Partners Inc. poll.
[2] *Source*: Data from a *Washington Post* poll.
[3] *Source*: Data from a CBS News poll.

This evidence suggests that public opinion concerning political leaders responsible for reforming Medicare in 1995 shifted during the later stages of the debate. The following section explains how media coverage could have influenced these shifts in opinion.

LINKING CRITICAL TONE IN MEDIA COVERAGE OF MEDICARE WITH PUBLIC OPINION

Media's influence on public opinion derives from its ability to choose what to relay to the public and how. When constructing articles or stories concerning Medicare, journalists decide which sources to use, which facts or opinions to present, and the tone of the message. The resulting choices convey to the audience a package of information that may include a picture of the actions and rhetoric espoused by political actors during debate, opinions concerning the desirability of proposed policy options, or factual information about the financing, benefits, and costs of the Medicare program. This information is then incorporated into the public's assessments of efforts to reform Medicare.

For example, the problems affecting the Medicare program have multiple causes that necessitate careful decisions about how to discuss reform options. During the last major debate concerning fundamental changes to Medicare, a news story about proposed Medicare reforms began by suggesting that "everyone" believed that the government faced critical Medicare issues. The correspondent for this story suggested that Medicare's problems would continue to worsen due to "...people living longer and using more expensive medical technology...." (ABC News 1995). The story also could have presented the following explanations for Medicare's projected financing problems: the future swell in the number of Medicare recipients that will be caused by the aging of the "baby-boomers;" the anticipated decrease in the ratio of workers to recipients that will accompany the "boomers;" or an inadequate payroll tax rate. Someone—an editor, producer, or journalist—chose the explanations to associate with Medicare's problems in this story; and, based on current research, the resulting messages likely affected the salience of these explanations with the public and primed the public to expect policies that addressed them.

This study focuses on an aspect of media coverage that, along with the measure of trust in leaders' ability to handle Medicare, incorporates assessments of both policy and political aspects of reform: the critical tone directed toward the policy and political positions of major newsmakers. The indicator of criticism used in the present study and subsequently defined measures whether or not a journalist's interpretations of the positions of the newsmaker are supportive. Despite the subjective nature of measures of tone, research suggests that media criticism is an important determinant of the public's support for government policies and policymakers.[8]

HYPOTHESIS

The importance of media criticism and shifts in the public's support during Medicare reform lead to the following hypothesis:

Hypothesis: Shifts in the amount and percentage of critical coverage of President Clinton and the Republican leadership during Medicare reform in 1995-96 were negatively correlated with shifts in the public's confidence in their ability to address Medicare's problems.

DATA AND METHODS

The data for this study were collected from a variety of newspapers and network evening news broadcasts.[9] Included among the print media are three national and two regional daily newspapers included to represent a range of perspectives. *USA Today* is a general interests paper with the second largest average daily circulation of any newspaper in the United States (American Newspaper Publishers Association 1996). The *New York Times (NYT)*, a nationally recognized paper, is also the local and regional paper for the largest city in the United States and a source of news for the nation's political and policy "elite." Along with the *Washington Post* and other sources, the *NYT* belongs to a small group of opinion leaders among media that affects coverage decisions made in other media (Jamieson and Campbell 1992). The *Washington Post* provides a unique view of national politics. As Linsky noted, "To government insiders, the news in Washington mean to a considerable degree what appears in the *Washington Post*. As Phillip 'Sam' Hughes, who has held several major policy positions, put it, 'The best way to find out what's going on in this town at any given moment is to read the goddamn paper, the *Post* notably."[10] Finally, articles from two large regional newspapers (*Dallas Morning News* and *St. Petersburg Times*) were also included to expand the geographic and diversity of the sources of data.

Every article or broadcast news story that contained the word "Medicare" and was disseminated in each of these publications was collected from the LEXIS-NEXIS database.[11] The review began with coverage published in the three national sources beginning on March 1, 1995 and ending on January 30, 1996. The regional coverage included in this study begins on September 1, 1995 and concludes on January 30, 1996.

Broadcast news stories from the three major networks were collected from the Vanderbilt University Television News Archives. All stories shown from March 1, 1995 through January 31, 1996 as a part of ABC World News Tonight, CBS Evening News, and the NBC Nightly News that contained references to Medicare were included in the dataset.

The data consist of all media coverage including a reference to Medicare from the print and broadcast media sources previously described. Once the data were gathered, coders reviewed each article or story and all articles that were letters to the editor, obituaries, or news previews were omitted. The remaining sample includes 1,712 articles or stories. While analyzing the coverage, the coders determined that 49 percent of it contained only a passing reference to Medicare.[12] These 833 articles or stories, which were coded and included in the database, were excluded from this analysis. The remaining coverage reports on Medicare or Medicare and Medicaid as the primary topic. The final distribution by source of the 879 articles or stories described in this study is displayed in Table 3.

Table 3: Distribution of Media Stories about Medicare in 1995-96 by Source

Media Source	All Articles or Stories with a Reference to Medicare		Articles or Stories with Medicare as a Primary Topic	
	N	percent	N	percent
New York Times	444	25.9	216	24.6
Washington Post	592	34.6	296	33.7
USA Today	247	14.4	104	11.8
Dallas Morning News	163	9.5	74	8.4
St. Petersburg Times	114	6.7	65	7.4
ABC *World News Tonight*	55	3.2	47	5.4
CBS *Evening News*	47	2.8	32	3.6
NBC *Nightly News*	50	2.9	45	5.1
Total	1,712		879	

Intercoder reliability measures the extent to which coders, operating autonomously, code or classify an article or story in the same way. Tests for the reliability of the coding were performed and no significant recurring differences were found. The full text of 20 percent of all articles or stories were coded by two coders and intercoder agreement rates were 90 percent or greater for all analyzed variables. A rate of at least 93 percent was reached for the coding of subjective variables, such as the tone of the coverage. To determine the reliability of the coding, two coders coded one-third of the articles or stories containing subjective measures.

KEY CONCEPTS AND VARIABLES

In this study, four variables describing the information media reported to the public during the Medicare reform debates of 1995-96 are linked to changes in public opinion concerning Medicare reform: tone of coverage, primary topic, context of reform, and impact of reform. The following information define and describe these variables along with other relevant concepts, such as "story type" and "newsmaker".

The first variable of interest is "story type." Media coverage includes a variety of packages for information. News reports (45 percent of the coverage included in this study) and accompanying background information (23 percent of Medicare coverage) are not the only mechanisms through which media convey to the public information about various aspects of Medicare.[13] Print media also publish editorials, commentary, and opinion pieces inspired by recent news events (22 percent of Medicare coverage) that present the policy or political position of the media outlet or author.[14] While these articles, usually contained in the editorial section, are not held to the same objective journalistic standards as news reports, they do present facts and arguments intended to affect public opinion about Medicare policy and political leaders.[15] The news reports, editorials, commentary, and opinion pieces that compose the "coverage" described in this analysis provide a broad range of media articles and stories conveying criticism of newsmakers' efforts to reform Medicare in 1995-96.

The predominant newsmaker in coverage of Medicare, the second variable of interest, was a member of Congress or of the Executive Branch of the federal government.[16] Fifty-six percent of Medicare coverage contained a member of Congress as the primary newsmaker and 20 percent included members of the Executive Branch in that role (Figure 2). Only three percent of all Medicare coverage (included in the Other category in the chart) did not have a primary newsmaker.

Among articles or stories in which a member of Congress was the major newsmaker, 53 percent focused on various representatives of the Republican party and an additional seven percent on Speaker Newt Gingrich, specifically. President Clinton was the newsmaker in 59 percent of the coverage in which a member of the Executive Branch was the key political actor.

Five percent of all stories about Medicare contained a major newsmaker from a group interested in Medicare, such as the American Association of Retired Persons, and an additional seven percent focused on representatives of the medical community, such as the American Medical Association.

During this debate, the Republican leadership and President Clinton were the primary proponents of plans to reform Medicare.

Accordingly, media reported and commented on their actions and rhetoric, and the public's support for their efforts. The remaining presentations focus on coverage and public opinion concerning President Clinton and Republicans in Congress.

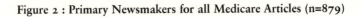

Figure 2 : Primary Newsmakers for all Medicare Articles (n=879)

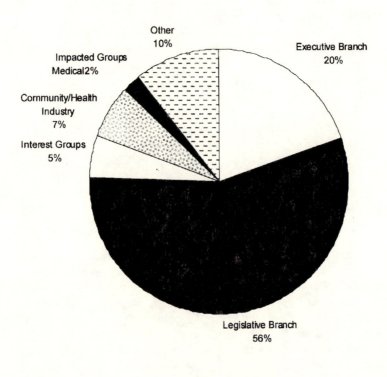

The "tone of coverage" variable indicates the tone directed toward the newsmakers. Each story or article could have a primary and a secondary newsmaker.[17] Accordingly, each article or story could be coded for tone that applied to at most two newsmakers. Sixty-seven percent of coverage with a primary newsmaker was also coded for a secondary newsmaker.

Coders evaluated journalists' interpretations or innuendoes concerning newsmakers, and coverage was deemed "not neutral" if the interpretations, whether positive (praise) or negative (critical), are presented in a ratio to the opposite view of at least 2:1. Coverage was primarily critical of or in praise of policy matters or political positions.[18]

Thirteen percent of all coverage of Medicare was critical of President Clinton and three percent was in praise of President Clinton's policy or political position (Figure 3). Sixty-five percent of the coverage did not include President Clinton as a newsmaker. In contrast, 39 percent of Medicare coverage was critical of the Republican leadership and four percent of coverage was in praise of Republicans (Figure 3). Only 22 percent of Medicare coverage did not have the Republican leadership as a major or secondary newsmaker.

During this debate, among coverage that could persuade the public via its tone (i.e. coverage that was not neutral), criticism was the largest component. Accordingly, this analysis focuses on explaining and understanding the impact of critical coverage that could negatively influence the public's support. When contemplating strategies for influencing media coverage to affect public opinion, newsmakers can consider ways to reduce the level of criticism or to increase the level of praise within their coverage. Efforts to reduce criticism would impact the type of tone that was most likely to be received by the public, which would provide more opportunity for influence.

One way to view media's assessment of newsmakers is to examine a measure of the intensity of the critical coverage relative to neutral coverage or praise. Figure 4 shows the percentage of President Clinton and the Republican leadership's coverage that was critical. For example, in August, 30 percent of media coverage that highlighted the Republican leadership as newsmakers was critical of Republicans. An alternative measure of the tone of coverage, the number of articles with critical coverage of each newsmaker, will be discussed in more detail in the discussion of the results (Figure 9).

Three variables are used to describe how the likelihood of critical coverage varies: the primary topic, context, and impact of reform. The impact of these variables is explored because representatives of political parties and the branches of the federal government, especially the President, are a significant source of information and news events for media (Jamieson and Campbell 1992). Thus, newsmakers have some direct influence on how media cover these factors. The following information describes these variables and their occurrence in the coverage.

Figure 3: Tone of Articles for Each Group of Newsmakers

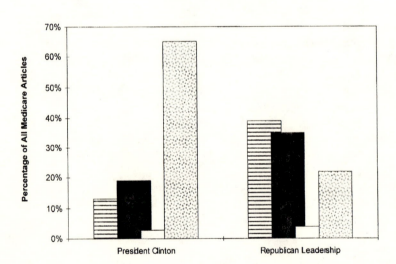

Figure 4: Change in Intensity of the Critical Coverage of Major Newsmakers

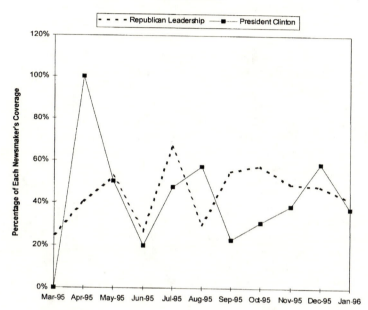

Month

Media coverage of Medicare could discuss as the primary topic various aspects of the program or tie the program to other issues. The range of Medicare topics was coded into five categories subsequently described.[19]

Topics in the first category, labeled **Medicare Program**, include Medicare program elements or descriptions (e.g., managed care, medical savings accounts, or a voucher system) and Medicare eligibility (e.g., age or other eligibility requirements). For example, an April 30, 1995 article entitled, "Look Before Leaping Into 'Managed' Medicare" discusses the advantages and disadvantages of increasing the enrollment of Medicare recipients in managed care systems such as HMOs (Crenshaw 1995).

The second category, labeled **Medicare Funding**, contains coverage in which Medicare funding issues, such as fraud and abuse, monthly premiums to recipients, or changes in spending are the primary topic. For example, a May 1, 1995 article entitled, "Medicare's Going Broke – and Fast!" uses the White House

Conference on Aging as a lead-in to discuss the financing of Medicare's two funds, Part A and Part B (Snow 1995).[20]

Other Medicare topics, such as polling data, the demographics of older Americans, or prescription drug benefits comprise the third category, labeled **Medicare Miscellaneous.** For example, an April 1995 article entitled, "A Medicare Dilemma: More 65 Year-Olds" discusses the impact of the impending influx of "baby-boomers" on future Medicare spending (The *Washington Post* 1995).

The next category is the final group of articles or stories for which Medicare is the only primary topic. The **Medicare Politics** category captures political events or actions focusing only on Medicare and including candidate rhetoric, legislative debate, or public committee hearings. For example, an October article beginning with the headline, "Two Key Panels Back GOP on Medicare..." describes the legislative process and debate surrounding the consideration of Medicare proposals in the House Ways and Means and Commerce committees (Dodge 1995).

The final category, labeled **Other Medicare,** includes coverage that presents information focusing on Medicare and at least one other significant topic. One method for determining the primary topic of an article is to note the topic(s) included in the headline or lead paragraph. For the examples used for the first four categories, the Medicare program is the only topic in the headline. In comparison, coverage in this category may not have Medicare as the lead topic and may describe aspects of the Medicare program as related to the other major topic of the article or story. For example, a May 9, 1995 broadcast with the headline, "Senate Republicans Present Plan to Balance Budget..." briefly highlights politicians' efforts to balance the federal budget. Changes to Medicare were one component of the changes needed to meet that goal and presented in the story (CBS 1995).

A large majority of Medicare topics conveyed to the public during this debate were from the Medicare Politics and Other Medicare categories (Figure 5). Three-fourths of the coverage (75 percent) was evenly divided between coverage in which Medicare Politics was the primary topic (38 percent of all Medicare coverage) and coverage in which Other Medicare was the primary topic (37 percent of all Medicare coverage). Only eight percent of the coverage about Medicare focused primarily on topics in the

Medicare Program category, 12 percent on Medicare Funding, and five percent on Medicare Miscellaneous.

Two variables in this analysis are used to develop a more specific view of other topics linked with the Medicare program in Other Medicare. First, each article or story was coded to capture ad-hoc issues or unpredicted events that received a high profile in media coverage for a finite period of time during the period of this study (i.e., a big event). A majority of the coverage in the Other Medicare category also included big events related to the legislative process in which Medicare was embroiled. About one-fourth of articles and stories in this category (23 percent) was related to big events such as federal funding or budget negotiations. Eighteen percent of this coverage was linked to the balanced budget debates, and another 17 percent was linked to the government shutdown. In summary, 68 percent of Other Medicare coverage was introduced with events from the legislative process. Additionally, 55 percent of the secondary topics connected with Other Medicare coverage were political activities.[21] A large majority of those activities were connected to proposals to change the funding of Medicare within the context of the budget debates.

Because the Other Medicare category is dominated by topics related to political events, Medicare Politics and Other Medicare capture similar ideas. The primary distinction between the two categories is the emphasis on Medicare. For the Medicare Politics coverage, Medicare is the only major topic in the coverage, and the article or story also discusses a political event or actor. In the Other Medicare coverage, Medicare shares the spotlight with another major topic that is most often a political event. Although for this study these two categories are similar, throughout this analysis they are described separately to reflect the fact that a sizable minority of the other topics are not related to politics.

Figure 5. Primary Topics

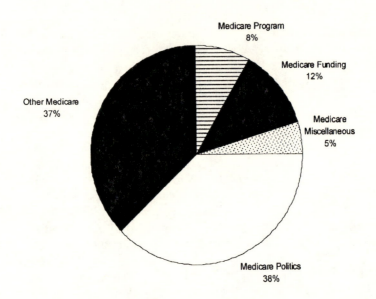

During these debates, the ways in which proposals to change Medicare were framed, another variable of interest, likely primed the public's support for these reforms and their sponsors. Avoiding the bankruptcy of the Medicare program and balancing the federal budget were the contexts used most frequently by media to explain the need for reform. About one-quarter of the coverage (26 percent) explained the need for reform in terms of avoiding bankruptcy or saving Medicare, 24 percent justified reforms with the need to balance the budget or reduce the federal deficit, and 31 percent contained two or more contextual elements (Figure 6).[22]

The contexts presented in the coverage helped to explain why proposals to reform Medicare were on the political agenda. The impact variable designates the manner in which the article or story examines the impact of potential Medicare reform. Sixty-nine percent of all Medicare coverage focused on the political impact of proposed reform (Figure 7). Eighteen percent of all coverage highlighted the groups or communities affected by possible reforms, such as disabled or older Americans.

Figure 6: Contexts Used to Justify Medicare Reform

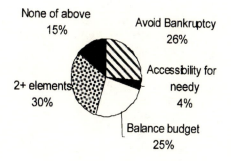

None of above
15%

Avoid Bankruptcy
26%

Accessibility for
needy
4%

Balance budget
25%

2+ elements
30%

Figure 7: Impacts Associated with Proposed Medicare Reforms

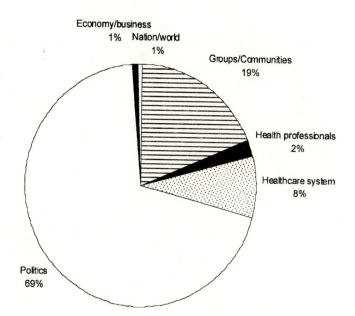

Economy/business
1%   Nation/world
1%

Groups/Communities
19%

Health professionals
2%

Healthcare system
8%

Politics
69%

RESULTS

The argument tested with this analysis suggests that the relative amount of critical coverage of the Republican leadership or President Clinton will be negatively correlated with shifts in the public's support for their ability to make decisions concerning Medicare. Two variables describe the amount of critical coverage. The first variable is a two-month rolling average of the percentage of critical coverage that smoothes some of the volatility of coverage in early months. Using a measure of the average level of criticism that would affect public opinion also assumes that opinions are informed by both the most recent information and an accumulation of information over time. The second variable is the number of articles coded for critical coverage of the two major newsmakers, and is included in the analysis in order to compare the results with other studies linking public opinion and media coverage. Figures 8-9 provide evidence that addresses the hypothesis.

Figure 8: Two Month Rolling Average of the Percentage of Each Newsmaker's Coverage that was Critical

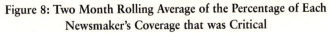

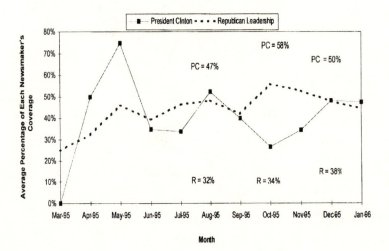

Figure 9. Change in the Amount of Critical Coverage for Newsmakers

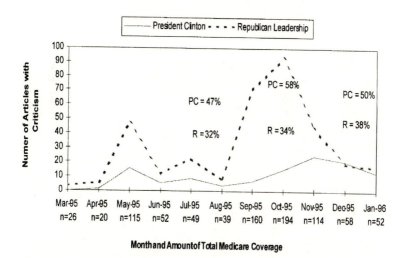

For President Clinton, approval of his capabilities did shift with changes in the average percentage of critical coverage, which supports the hypothesis. For October 1995, 58 percent of the public trusted President Clinton to make decisions about Medicare, which was an eleven point increase in support compared with his level of support at the end of August (Table 2). The higher level of support for the President at the end of October is accompanied by a relatively low average of critical coverage (27 percent), which is a 25 point decrease from the average level of criticism affecting the August measure of support. Additionally, at the beginning of January the percentage of Americans who trusted the President with Medicare was 50 percent. This rating was preceded by a higher average percentage of critical coverage in December (48 percent) than in October. In summary, shifts in the percentage of Americans who trusted President Clinton's decisions concerning Medicare were negatively correlated with changes in the average percentage of the President's coverage that was critical.

The monthly number of critical articles or stories for President Clinton was small compared with the volume of critical coverage for the Republican leadership. President Clinton's amount of critical coverage ranged from zero and one in March and April, respectively, to 25 in November. This measure provides mixed support for the hypothesis. The October increase in support for President Clinton was accompanied by an increase in the amount of critical coverage, which does not support the hypothesis. In August, four articles or stories were critical of President Clinton. By October, the amount had more than tripled (15 articles or stories). At the beginning of January, 25 and 12 critical articles or stories in November and December, respectively, had preceded the opinion measure.

For the Republican leadership, the correlation between shifts in public opinion and changes in the average percentage of critical coverage is not consistent (Figure 8). At the end of August, 32 percent of the public trusted Republicans in Congress to make decisions about Medicare (Table 2). A relatively average level of criticism in August (average of 48 percent) accompanied this measure of public opinion. Compared with the critical coverage of Republicans in July and August, the average amount of criticism for September and October was relatively high (average of 56 percent), in fact, the highest average percentage of the entire period. Contrary to predictions of the hypothesis, the accompanying measure of support for the Republican leadership did not change significantly from August to October. In December, the end of the debates about Medicare in 1995, the average percentage of critical coverage of Republican leadership was 50 percent. The trend toward decreasing average levels of critical coverage in December and January is accompanied by a small and significant increase in the percentage of Americans who trusted the Republican leadership with Medicare, which supports the hypothesis.

The volume measure of criticism for the Republican leadership has the same patterns of relationships as did the average percentage measure. High levels of critical coverage in September and December (71 and 93, respectively) did not correlate with the lack of a shift in public support for the Republican leadership in October. The increase in support at the beginning of January was preceded by large decreases in the volume of critical coverage in November and December when compared with levels of criticism in the preceding two months.

In summary, changes in the two-month average of the level of critical coverage for President Clinton clearly correlated with shifts in the amount of public support for his ability to handle Medicare. The link between the average level of critical coverage for the Republican leadership and the amount of public support for their reform efforts provided mixed support for the hypothesis. Finally, results describing the relationship between public support and the volume measure of critical coverage also provided mixed support for the hypothesis.

Based on the previous results, newsmakers should have some concern about the mix of tone used to describe their reform efforts. Next, aspects of coverage influenced by newsmakers are linked to variation in the amount of their critical coverage.

Probit regressions reveal how the foci of coverage explain variation in the likelihood of critical coverage for President Clinton and the Republican leadership (Table 4). For President Clinton, compared with Medicare topics and contexts that are policy-related, political factors associated with the President tended to have higher levels of criticism. Compared with policy related topics (Medicare Program, Medicare Funding, and Medicare Miscellaneous categories), topics from the Other Medicare category had a 12 percentage point greater likelihood of being critical of President Clinton. Compared with coverage in which reform was justified as a way of saving the Medicare program, discussions of balancing the budget were seven percentage points more likely to be critical. Finally, coverage of President Clinton that focused on the political impact of potential reforms were eight percentage points more likely to be critical than coverage with impacts associated with individuals or communities.

Table 4: Probit Parameter Estimates for Likelihood of Critical Coverage

	President Clinton	Republican Leadership	President Clinton	Republican Leadership
	Parameter Est. (SE)	Parameter Est. (SE)	DY/Dx	DY/Dx
Intercept	-2.19* 0.24	-0.80* 0.14	—	—
primary topic				
Medicare Program (ref)				
Medicare Politics	0.37 0.20	0.44 0.13	0.07	0.17*
Other Medicare	0.60* 0.20	0.10 0.13	0.12	0.04
context for reform				
Saving Medicare (ref)				
Accessibility of needy	0.40 0.38	0.72* 0.24	0.09	0.28*
Balancing the federal budget	0.37 0.18	0.18 0.14	0.06*	0.07
Two or more contexts	0.03 0.14	0.00 0.12	0.00	0.00
No context	0.01 0.22	-0.09 0.15	0.00	-0.03
impact of reform				
Individuals/groups (ref)				
Health professionals/system	-0.46 0.42	0.08 0.18	-0.06	0.03
Politics	0.54* 0.19	0.26* 0.13	0.08*	0.10*
Other	0.52 0.46	-0.21 0.38	0.12	-0.08
Model X^2	64.18*	39.83*		

The primary topics and contexts that explain variation in the level of criticism for the Republican leadership vary somewhat from those that explain criticism for President Clinton. For Republicans, coverage in which Medicare Politics topics were the focus were 17 percentage points more likely to be critical than topics related to policy related aspects of the Medicare program. Discussion in which accessibility for the needy or reducing the federal deficit were the justifications for reform were 29 percentage points more likely to be critical than coverage of justifications related to saving Medicare.[23] Finally, in the only result similar to the effect for President Clinton, discussions of the political impact of potential reforms were 10 percentage points more likely to contain criticism of Republicans than discussions of the impact on individuals or the community.

DISCUSSION/IMPLICATIONS

The purpose of this study was to provide insights into how media may affect future efforts to reform Medicare and how newsmakers may affect media's impact. The results suggest that media may affect Medicare policy outcomes via its relationship with public opinion. The public's attitudes toward Medicare throughout these debates may rely, in part, on how media prime expectations concerning particular policymakers grappling with them via the tone of coverage.

During the 1995 debate concerning fundamental changes to Medicare, the Republican leadership was the predominant newsmaker and coverage focusing on this group was more often than not critical of their policy or political positions. The two-month average percentage of critical coverage for Republicans shown in Figure 8 suggests that their share of critical coverage was a fairly stable upward trend until October, the height of media attention during the debate, and then headed downward in the last few months. From a different perspective, October also had the largest number of articles or stories (93) and the largest percentage of all stories in a month (50 percent) that were critical of the Republican leadership. Based on these results, media were more likely to be more critical of Republican leadership at a time during the debate when they were also more likely to include the Republican leadership in coverage. Links between shifts in critical tone and shifts in public opinion between August 1995 to January 1996 were not consistent. Contrary to expectations, the peak in the amount and mix of critical tone for the Republican leadership did not correspond to a decrease in their support.

An examination of only Republican or President Clinton's support suggests that the volume of coverage for both groups and the average level for Republicans were not correlated with their support. However, a closer look at the shifts in support suggests a different story. At the end of August, 21 percent of the public did not trust the capabilities of either Republicans or President Clinton with regard to Medicare. By October, only eight percent of the public had not made a choice. Of the twelve percent of the public who shifted to one of the newsmakers, only two percentage points of them supported Republicans. This shift was accompanied by the high levels of coverage critical of Republicans previously described. While the increase in the Republicans' critical coverage may not have been negatively correlated with the lack of change in their support in October, it seemed to be associated with Republicans not being able to take advantage of increased media attention that helped undecided Americans to make a choice.

President Clinton was also a major newsmaker, but not as often as were Republicans. Both the average percentage of his criticism and his support shifted significantly across the three measures, suggesting a negative correlation. Combined, these results suggest that policymakers concerned with how the public will perceive their efforts to reform Medicare should systematically monitor the tone of their coverage and seek ways to reduce the amount of their critical coverage.

For President Clinton, reducing the relative amount of criticism would have meant focusing speeches, events, and political rhetoric on the policy aspects of his positions. For Republicans, the majority of subjects that would have reduced criticism were policy-related; however, one of the policy-related items in their coverage did not receive less criticism than the corresponding political item. For Republicans, coverage that focused on saving the Medicare program was just as likely to be critical as coverage focusing on balancing the federal budget. This result may indicate media's skepticism of the Republicans' reform proposals. The media were just as critical of their efforts to save Medicare as they were of the suggestion that their efforts to change Medicare were motivated by their goal of balancing the budget.

Based on these results, policy experts who want to affect the level of criticism directed toward policy proponents should promote events that focus media attention on the policy debate and ensure that prominent political actors are armed with political rhetoric that also promotes a particular policy message.

This content analysis expands our understanding of the topics, contexts, and impacts highlighted in coverage of major Medicare reform. Additionally, no other published study has linked the level of critical coverage of major newsmakers during a health policy debate with public support for the newsmakers and used multivariate analysis to explain the variation in the level of criticism. The results of this study could be enhanced according to the following suggestions.

Descriptive statistics, which currently are the primary analytical method for content analysis, are generally suggestive of relationships that should be further explained with more sophisticated analytical techniques. A multivariate analysis of changes in opinion about Medicare policy and newsmakers that incorporated measures of media coverage would determine whether coverage explains variations in public opinion controlling for other factors that may have caused the shifts in support. For example, the increased coverage during that period may have provided undecided Americans with enough information about President Clinton's general, alternative plan for changing Medicare for them to support his judgment.

Additionally, research including more measures of public opinion could help to pinpoint when attitudes shifted. Without more measures, it is difficult to discern whether or not media influenced the amount of critical coverage, reflected the public's changing attitudes, or some combination of both. Finally, more detailed coding of the content of coverage would facilitate a more comprehensive analysis explaining the tone of coverage as well as other types of changes in public opinion. For example, coding that captured the words media used to explain specific policy proposals could be linked to support for the policy proposals.

NOTES

[1] For evidence linking public opinion with policy outcomes, see Page and Shapiro (1992) and Monroe (1998).

[2] For an example of the role of public opinion polls during debates of Medicare policy, see Himelfarb (1995).

[3] Media are defined as means of communication that reach the general public and carry advertising (Jamieson and Campbell 1992). Print and electronic (together known as broadcast) are the two basic types of media. Media include television, radio, newspapers, and magazines.

[4] According to 1995 Media Consumption Surveys conducted by the Pew Center for the People and the Press, 69 percent of Americans reported reading any newspaper regularly and 78 percent watched any television news program regularly. Sixty-five percent of Americans reported regularly watching a major television network evening news program (Pew Center for the People and the Press, 1999).

Capturing the impact of media on public opinion is a difficult and controversial task. Media messages are among a myriad of influences on citizens' cognitive processes as they make decisions about their own political opinions and behavior. Despite these difficulties, researchers have presented convincing evidence suggesting that media messages are received and processed by the audience and have an impact on their opinions via influence on the priorities they give to issues, their perceptions of political life and political actors, and attributions of responsibility. For examples, see Rogers and Dearing (1988), Page, Shapiro and Dempsey (1987), Iyengar (1991), Ansolabehere, Behr, and Iyengar (1993), and Krosnick and Kinder (1990).

A recent study links the content of media coverage to changes in the opinion of Americans 65 years of age and older (Fan and Norem 1992). Using a model incorporating scores for the persuasive content of paragraphs discussing the MCEA and the likely impact of this coverage on opinion over time, they calculated an expected time trend for public opinion. The results demonstrate that mass media stories can forecast trends in public opinion, in this case for older Americans, and suggest a strong link between media coverage of Medicare and public opinion.

[5] Unless otherwise noted, descriptions of the Medicare proposals and legislative debate are based on *Congressional Quarterly Almanac: 104th Congress, 1st Session...1995, Volume LI.*

6   As the majority party Republicans consistently rebuffed Congressional Democrats' efforts to amend the Republican proposal or to introduce their own proposal.

7   While having only three measures limits this study to results that are suggestive of the true relationship between public opinion and media coverage, I argue that the results of these comparisons provide an important underpinning for future research. Any study of public opinion during a policy debate is constrained by surveys conducted by a variety of organizations. In this case, I chose these questions, in part, because they occurred throughout the debate with the same question wording and response categories. Questions that asked about similar concepts with different question wordings or small sample sizes were not included because I wanted to maximize the validity of any shifts that occurred.

8   See Reeves (1997) and Fan and Norem (1992) for evidence linking the tone of media coverage to the public's attitudes.

9   Researchers at the Kaiser Family Foundation and Princeton Survey Research Associates (PSRA) developed the data for this study. PSRA had primary responsibility for data collection and coding.

10   Linsky, Martin, *Impact: How the Press Affects Federal Policymaking* (New York: W.W. Norton and Company, 1986), 3.

11   The data collection also included references to Medicaid. Future analysis of the data will compare coverage of Medicare and Medicaid, health policy programs that inspire different political dynamics, during this time period. I received specific information concerning data collection and coding for this study from Mollyann Brodie at the Kaiser Family Foundation and Lee Ann Brady at PSRA. The format for presenting information about data collection is based on similar sections in Brodie, Brady, and Altman (1998).

12   Coverage in which at least one-third of the presentation was not about Medicare are not included in this analysis.

13   Media disseminate many types of information in many forms. Whether or not the vehicle that delivers the messages about Medicare is news, an editorial, or a sitcom affects the intended purpose of the information and how the audience perceives the information and incorporates it into their assessments of the Medicare program. Therefore, the nature of the program or article containing health information is an important variable to consider when conducting and considering the results of media analysis. While many stories convey information to the public about places, people, and events related to Medicare, researchers tend to focus on the impact of stories intended to inform the public on the latest events: hard news. Hard

news can be defined as "...the report of an event that happened or was disclosed within the previous twenty-four hours and treats an issue of ongoing concern" (Jamieson and Campbell 1992, 31). The event reported may not be recent, but the story must contain some new information. However, all events that happen within twenty-four hours of a newscast are not reported as news. Along with dimensions, such as time and place, that distinguish types of stories, characteristics of the event also determine whether or not media will report the story as news. Media research highlights several qualities that deem an event newsworthy. Events covered by media will have some combination of the following factors: connection to a personality, drama and conflict, an action or observable occurrence, an idea or event that is novel or deviant, or a link to issues of ongoing interest.

[14] The remaining 10 percent of Medicare coverage included lengthy interviews, personality profiles, news analysis, and bullet items.

[15] See Dalton, Beck, and Huckfeldt (1998) for evidence linking the editorial content of local newspapers with their readers' preferences for presidential candidates.

[16] A group may also be coded a primary leader, e.g., the Democratic Leadership in the House of Representatives. For a newsmaker to be primary, at least one-third of the article or story must have related to the newsmaker.

[17] A primary newsmaker had to accompany a secondary newsmaker. For a newsmaker to be secondary, at least one-fifth of the article or story must have related to the newsmaker.

[18] Less than one percent of all criticism or praise was for personal qualities.

[19] For Medicare to be the primary topic, at least one-third of the article or story must have discussed Medicare.

[20] Part A of Medicare primarily provides insurance for hospital stays. Part B primarily funds physicians care.

[21] Once the major topic was coded, a secondary topic was also coded if the topic constituted at least 20 percent of the discussion within an article or story.

[22] The specific elements included in this last group cannot be discerned from the coded variable. Presumably a significant element included in this category would also have been coded separately.

[23] This context category contains 34 stories or articles. Ninety-one percent of them concern accessibility for the needy, and 32 percent of those stories have both Medicare and Medicaid as the primary topic.

CHAPTER TWO

Political Knowledge

On numerous occasions, I have heard health policy experts interviewed on National Public Radio who have lamented the public's lack of understanding of policy-related concepts, such as risk associated with environmental hazards or disease. These experts assume that a public better educated about health issues would have different policy preferences, priorities, or willingness to pay for policy options. For example, a person who understands the fact that health services for children tend to yield larger long-term health benefits than the same investment in older Americans may be more willing to shift government resources currently used by older Americans to treatment of children. Similarly, interest groups, such as the American Association of Retired Persons, distribute information about health issues and programs to their members with the hope that the information will inform attitudes about policy proposals or other choices related to health issues.

This study investigates whether or not efforts to educate the public or segments of the public about a major health program, Medicare, would matter via an effect on policy preferences. Medicare is an ideal program for testing the effects of educating the public for several reasons. First, because Medicare is a significant health program that serves millions of older and disabled Americans, numerous policy experts and interest groups could benefit from understanding the impact of investments aimed at educating the public. Second, the financial issues facing Medicare ensure that lessons learned about the impact of information can be applied to debates in the near future. Finally, because this study attempts to explain support for policy proposals that were the focus of the last major attempt to reform Medicare, insights based on these results are likely to be directly applicable to some of the proposals that will be considered in the next round of Medicare reform.

The analysis begins with justification for relying on models and evidence from the field of political science to predict the role of information concerning Medicare policy. The next two sections describe the models and evidence linking information and public opinion that inform my hypotheses and the methods of this study. The subsequent sections describe the data for this study and the dependent and independent variables included in the analyses. The final sections contain results explaining how information is distributed among segments of the population, the impact of Medicare knowledge, and a discussion of the implications for policy outcomes and future research.

EXPLAINING THE ROLE OF INFORMATION IN PUBLIC OPINION FORMATION

As a health insurance program, decisions pertaining to Medicare's funding mechanisms, benefits, etc. are based on information reflecting the health needs of Medicare recipients, the current structure of the program, the costs of medical care, etc. Medicare is also a sizable portion of the federal budget, is supported by taxes paid by a large majority of Americans, and is the primary source of medical insurance for politically active older Americans (Moon 1997). As a result, federal politicians decide Medicare policy, and their decisions are also influenced by information pertaining to political ramifications, such as measures of public opinion. In summary, Medicare is both a policy and a political issue and two types of information inform decisions concerning the program: information about Medicare as a health program and information about the politics of Medicare policy decisions.[24]

Similarly, I contend that two types of information can influence the public's preferences for Medicare policy. One set of information is what many researchers refer to as political knowledge: factual information about political institutions or political actors, such as which political party controls Congress, the role of Congress, or which political party supports which policy alternative. The second type of information, described in more detail in a subsequent section, is specific to Medicare as a policy issue. The present study expands our understanding of information effects during political debates by focusing on the impact of policy-related information.

Because Medicare is an important political and policy issue, the models and evidence that I use to support this study come primarily from the political science literature. Based on this literature, I assume that knowledge of the political system, the political ramifications of Medicare reform proposals, and issue knowledge affect attitudes concerning Medicare politics and policy via the same mechanisms. Accordingly, the following models and evidence explaining why and how political information matters form the basis of understanding the role of information about the Medicare program during policy debates.

Information processing models embody theories that explain how people select political information, transform that information into beliefs or schema about political problems and the political system, and use that information to form evaluations and opinions. Three prominent examples of how political scientists have used information-processing theories to explain and confirm empirically the relationship between political knowledge and the formation of political attitudes are subsequently described.[25]

In the context of responding to a survey, Zaller (1992) describes the formation of opinions as outcomes of a process. People receive new political information (reception), decide whether to accept offered reasons for particular attitudes (acceptance), and choose from among the accepted reasons when answering survey questions (sample). Thus, respondents construct opinion statements "on-the-spot" primarily from ideas (inspired by news, conversations with friends, or recent personal experiences) that are most salient and accessible.[26]

Each individual's level of political knowledge affects the process of forming and expressing opinions in all of these stages. In the receptance stage, the level of knowledge about public affairs predicts awareness of an issue and cognitive engagement with an issue. The greater a person's level of cognitive engagement with an issue, the more likely he is to be exposed to and to comprehend (to receive) political messages concerning that issue. Differences in the reception of persuasive messages suggest differences in accessible considerations and, as a result, opinions. In the acceptance stage, people tend to resist arguments that are inconsistent with their political predispositions, but they do so only to the extent that they possess the contextual information necessary to perceive a relationship between the message and their predispositions. While those with less involvement in politics are less likely to receive political messages via media, they are more likely to accept those messages indiscriminately due to lack of information or cues that would enable them to compare persuasive messages with their own values and interests. In the final stage, when asked to respond to a survey question, highly knowledgeable people are more likely than people who have less knowledge to remember more ideas and considerations.

Sniderman, Brody, & Tetlock (1991) provide an alternative model for how citizens make political choices that is not entirely inconsistent with Zaller's explanation. Their model is based on the idea that specific knowledge about the wide array of issues and political institutions is not necessary for people to successfully ascertain their political preferences, especially for salient issues such as Medicare, the death penalty, abortion, etc. They argue that people can make reasonable political judgments without specific political knowledge by using judgmental heuristics (efficient ways to organize and simplify choices).

For Sniderman, Brody & Tetlock, varying levels of political sophistication indicate varying dependence on cognitive and affective reasoning when making political choices. For example, a less politically sophisticated person is more likely to consider policy choices based on affect-driven heuristics. The policy choices of a more politically sophisticated person are more likely to incorporate a comparison of costs and benefits or an opinion about the effectiveness of government with any affect towards relevant political parties or politicians supporting a particular policy option. Additionally, the most and least politically sophisticated people likely differ in the range of considerations recalled when making policy choices with more sophisticated people considering a larger range. In summary, more politically sophisticated people likely use different heuristics in different ways than less politically sophisticated people, which results in different likelihoods of support for particular policy options, *ceteris paribus*.

In this model, knowledge plays a role in determining a person's level of political sophistication. Incorporated into political sophistication are political awareness, political information, and comprehension of arguments supporting a policy issue. Thus, political information is one component of political sophistication that likely determines reliance on particular heuristics for public opinion formation.[27]

In the third model, Lodge, McGraw, and Stroh (1989), with further support from Lodge, Steenbergen, and Brau (1995), utilize underpinnings from research by Graber (1988) and the field of social psychology to develop an impression-driven information processing model. The memory-based models previously discussed assume that when a person is asked to evaluate a political candidate or issue he will recall the pros and cons available in memory. Empirical studies highlight the difficulty people have retrieving specific information, weighing evidence, and incorporating the evidence into an evaluation (For a review see Hastie and Park 1986). The on-line processing of the Lodge et al. model does not rely on accessing long-term memory for the retrieval of pertinent, specific information.

Lodge, Steenbergen, and Brau argue that processing is continual and judgments are updated as information is received. For example, let us consider how Jane may form a political opinion. Yesterday, Jane had not heard or read about a recommendation to raise the age of eligibility for Medicare from 65 to 67. Today she reads an article in the regional newspaper that provides a balanced discussion of the political and policy debates concerning this policy option. Upon completion of the article, Jane forms an opinion about this proposal. During the following week, Jane reads new information about Medicare's problems and the impact of changing the age of eligibility. At that time, she retrieves her existing opinion about the eligibility change from memory, makes adjustments, and stores the result in memory. The next day, Jane is asked to express her opinion on the proposal concerning the age of eligibility for Medicare. According to Lodge, et al., rather than retrieving all of the information that informed her original opinion and reconstructing her views, Jane will retrieve her latest summary judgment.

In this model of opinion formation, information has a key role that may not be reflected in the impact of retrievable knowledge. Once the specific political information is incorporated into the summary judgment the information may be forgotten while the influence of the information exists. For this study, a measure of knowledge presumably indicates some combination of the factual information the person received and incorporated into their assessments of the policy option and their ability to process the information and form an opinion. As knowledge varies from person to person, so may opinions.

Lodge, et al., (1989, 1995) also contend that both memory based and on-line processes produce public opinion and the particular process used depends on the goal of the person at the time of receiving the information. When faced with an immediate need to form an impression or make a judgment, a person will use an impression-model. When faced with the need to acquire as much information as possible (which is rare) or with no pressure to make a judgment, a person will store information in memory and retrieve and evaluate whatever information is available when asked or needed. Additionally, the combination of information processing that occurs likely depends on whether or not the respondent has an opinion about the issue before participating in the survey and on whether or not the information used to form the opinion is general or specific (McGraw and Pinney 1990).

Despite differing explanations for the evolution of survey responses, all three of these models incorporate the idea that information and the accumulation and processing of information (knowledge) is an important factor shaping the resulting opinion. The next section presents a range of empirical evidence linking political knowledge with political behavior and opinions.

EVIDENCE OF THE EFFECT OF POLITICAL INFORMATION

The nature of political information needed to support a democracy has been argued for decades. Some political scientists support Delli Carpini and Keeter's argument (1996) that, "...democracy functions best when its citizens are politically informed. Factual knowledge on such topics as the institutions and processes of government, current economic and social conditions, the major issues of the day, and the stands of political leaders on those issues assists citizens in discerning their individual and group interests, in connecting their interests to broader notions of the public good, and in effectively expressing these views via political participation....[A] broadly and equitably informed citizenry helps assure a democracy that is both responsive and responsible" (1).

In contrast, other political scientists contend that low levels of detailed political information in the electorate do not prevent the public from expressing their "true" preferences. Citizens rationally rely on cues and information shortcuts to make decisions that reflect their interests. The level of specific political information in the electorate is moot because the electorate acts as if it was informed. This argument essentially replaces detailed information about the political process and specific information about policy issues with information that is more easily accessible for the public. These political cues and shortcuts, particularly for voting, can come from opinion leaders (e.g., Neuman 1986) party identification (Robertson 1976), retrospective evaluations of the economy (Fiorina 1981), and personal evaluations of political figures and groups (Brady and Sniderman 1985; Conover and Feldman 1989). For example, Lupia (1994) demonstrates that California voters with low levels of specific political knowledge who relied on political cues from the positions of relevant actors in a referendum battle voted in a manner consistent with the votes of well informed voters with comparable socio-economic characteristics.[28]

Whether the knowledge is specific or general, supporters of each argument promote the idea that citizens rely on political information to differentiate among political choices. Because this information enables the public's choices to reflect their preferences, political information is likely a critical underpinning of democratic political systems.

Despite the strength of theoretical arguments supporting the need for a politically knowledgeable public, little research has been published to show empirically how political information or knowledge affects preferences for specific public policy. This paucity of evidence likely reflects the long-standing theoretical and empirical evidence establishing the fact that voters tend to be rather uninformed about politics and that public opinion tends to lack stability and consistency[29]

The low levels of political knowledge in the general public have not precluded tests of its effects. While no published analysis has linked political knowledge with public opinion concerning a specific health policy option, evidence demonstrating differences between the political behavior and attitudes of well informed adults and adults who are not well informed suggest that the link could be significant.

Researchers have found well informed Americans to be less supportive of incumbents (Alvarez and Franklin 1994; Sniderman, Brody, and Tetlock 1991), more likely to be affected by elite arguments during political discourse (Zaller 1992), and to react differently to the priming effects of media (Krosnick and Kinder 1990; Krosnick and Brannon 1993) or to the balance of persuasive messages conveyed via mass media during political campaigns (Zaller 1996).[30] In studies of political behavior, changes in the level of political knowledge in the public have been linked to shifts in electoral outcomes. For example, Bartels (1996) finds a significant difference between actual vote probabilities and the vote probabilities of a hypothetical, fully informed electorate in several recent presidential elections.[31] Finally, research that has examined the impact of information on public opinion suggests that informed citizens are more likely to have meaningful, stable attitudes and are better able to link personal interests with attitudes as expressed in public opinion surveys (Delli Carpini and Keeter 1996).

The next section incorporates lessons learned from the previously discussed models of opinion formation and empirical evidence to predict how knowledge of Medicare should affect preferences for Medicare policy.

HYPOTHESES AND METHODS

Based on the previously discussed models and evidence, knowledge of the Medicare program likely represents a combination of three factors that affect a person's evaluation of Medicare policy: factual information needed to assess the costs and benefits of the policy proposal, engagement in the policy debate, and cognitive ability (Bartels 1996).[32] Because factual information is the factor of interest to entities interested in educating the public and can be used to systematically predict patterns of information effects, the hypotheses for this study are based on the likely effect of factual information incorporated into evaluations of support for Medicare policy.

To compare the results with effects demonstrated with political information, three methods are used to test how information may matter in this study. In all cases, survey respondents are assumed to weigh the costs and benefits of each proposal based, in part, on factual information about the program similar to the information used in this study.

The first part of this study assumes that knowledge will have the same effect across different segments of the population. For example, any differences in support for Medicare managed care among Democrats that can be attributed to varying knowledge levels is assumed to be the same among men. This assumption leads to the following hypothesis:

Hypothesis 1: As an independent variable, knowledge will not have a significant effect on the likelihood of support for Medicare policy.

This hypothesis is based on evidence showing that the effect of information on voting behavior in presidential elections varies by socio-political groups (Bartels 1996). Additionally, I argue that some of the facts that a person needs to assess the personal impact of a policy based on their level of income should differ from the information needed to assess the impact based on their level of education. I also contend that the role of factual information in assessing the personal impact of a policy will also differ by socio-political characteristics. For example, for John to assess how raising the payroll tax may affect him based on his income, he may need to know the current payroll tax rate and amount, the proposed rate and amount, and what payroll taxes fund in Medicare. To assess the value of the tax based on his political affiliation, he may only need to know the position of his political party. For each case, the role of specific, factual information about Medicare differs.

The second part of this study allows for information to affect preferences via interactions with characteristics that predict Medicare policy preferences. The second hypothesis follows:

Hypothesis 2: Information will have a significant effect on the impact of each determinant of Medicare policy for which the group represented by the characteristic has a direct or sizable stake.

This hypothesis is based on the idea that for people with a potentially large stake or interest in the impact of a policy proposal shifts in support can be large. For example, Medicare beneficiaries poorly informed about aspects of Medicare may strongly oppose a voucher system. Once they understand more about how Medicare is funded or how Medicare would change with this new option, they may reassess the impact and their support may change to strong support. In comparison, based on the large number of years until she can take advantage of Medicare or little indirect experience with Medicare via her parents, a 30-year-old adult may have weak support for a voucher system. New information about Medicare will not change Medicare's current effect on her or her family and may only shift her support to weak opposition. In summary, among Medicare beneficiaries there may be a significant difference in the likelihood of support for a new voucher system for Medicare caused by additional information. Among younger Americans, there may be no significant difference in support based on knowledge.

The six Medicare policies considered in this study affect various segments of the population differently (e.g., the public or Medicare beneficiaries), and propose different mechanisms to reform Medicare (e.g., changing the organization of services or changing the costs of services). Thus, the stakes vary both by policy and by segment of the population. Table 5 shows my assessment of which groups have a stake or interest in a particular policy option based on costs and benefits to each group. I predict that each "yes" designates a significant interaction effect.

Table 5: Assesment of Groups That Have a Stake or Special Interest in
Particular Medicare Policy Proposals

Segment of the Population	Medicare Policy Proposals					
	Voucher	HMO, etc.	> Payroll Tax	Change Age Eligibility	< Benefits	> Premiums
50-64 years	mixed	mixed	mixed	mixed	mixed	mixed
65+ years	yes	yes	no	no	yes	yes
Democrats	yes	no	yes	no	yes	yes
Indepedent/other	no	no	no	no	no	no
Moderate	mixed	no	mixed	no	no	no
Liberal	yes	no	yes	no	no	no
African American	yes	no	mixed	mixed	no	no
Asian/other	yes	no	mixed	no	no	no
$25-50k income	yes	yes	yes	no	yes	yes
$50k+income	no	no	no	no	no	no
Some college education	yes	yes	no	no	mixed	mixed
College/graduate education	no	no	no	no	no	no
Men	no	no	no	mixed	no	no

Notes: yes = this group is impacted by the policy or has a particular interest in the position it represents, mixed = some members of the group are particularly affected or interested.

The third hypothesis uses the previous model to predict a general pattern for differences in the impact of general knowledge about Medicare compared with the impact of a subset of more specific knowledge about Medicare:

Hypothesis 3: The more specific set of knowledge will affect the impact of more determinants of Medicare policy than the index that includes a broader range of knowledge questions.

Specific information about Medicare, such as facts about funding of benefits, is likely given to the public via mechanisms that differ from more general information. Also, people who remember specific information concerning Medicare likely have a particular interest in Medicare. Thus, people well informed about Medicare benefits likely differ somewhat from people who are well informed about more general aspects of Medicare, and the impact of the two sets of information will likely differ.

Based on the idea that knowledge matters and different sets of information matter differently, the third part of this study examines the impact of having a public with preferences that mirror the preferences of people who are well informed.

Hypothesis 4: Educating the public about Medicare will significantly changed its likelihood of support for Medicare policies. Additionally, the shifts in support caused by the general set of information will differ from those caused by the more specific set of information.

To test this hypothesis, the public's predicted probability of support for each policy is calculated. This likelihood of support is compared with the predicted probability of support for the public that is calculated using parameter estimates calculated for well informed adults only.

DATA[33]

The survey that created the data for this study was designed by researchers from the Kaiser Family Foundation and the Harvard School of Public Health's Department of Health Policy and Management and was conducted by Louis Harris and Associates, Inc. (Blendon 1995). The data represent the results from 1,383 telephone interviews conducted with adults 18 years of age or older between May 31 and June 5, 1995. The sample consists of 1,076 adults and an oversample of 307 people 65 years of age or older. In total, 548 people 65 years old or older were interviewed, and, unless indicated otherwise, their responses are weighted to the group's proportion among the national adult population.

The Harris National Telephone Sample for this survey was selected by a sampling process that ensures representation of households in central city, suburban, and rural areas within the 48 continental United States. The sample was generated from random digit dial procedures and designed to ensure equal representation of adults in households with telephones.[34]

When interpreting the results please keep two factors in mind (Blendon 1995). First, telephone surveys tend to underrepresent the views of people in the population who are less likely to have telephones, particularly people with small incomes. The 1993 American Housing Survey estimates that seven percent of households in the United States were without telephone service in 1993 (U.S. Government Printing Office 1996). Second, findings based on public opinion surveys are subject to sampling and nonsampling error. Based on the size of this sample, one can say with 95 percent confidence that the error attributable to random sampling could be approximately +/- three percent. The primary source of nonsampling error that may affect the external validity of the results is nonresponse bias.[35]

DESCRIPTIVE RESULTS

Knowledge is the range of factual, accurate information about an issue that is stored in long-term memory (adapted from Delli Carpini and Keeter 1996). Policy experts, media, or interest groups could increase the public's level of knowledge about Medicare with a wide range of information. The survey used for this study asks a small subset of possible questions that could be labeled "Medicare Program Knowledge."

In order to narrow the focus and implications of this study, I classify Medicare program knowledge into two categories: aggregate and specific.[36] On an aggregate level, one can know about Medicare's history, financing mechanisms, eligibility requirements, costs, benefits, etc. This type of information captures an understanding of Medicare in total. On a more individual level, one can also know specifics about the program that relate to individual experiences or the experiences of one's family and friends. For example, one can know which providers in the community are Medicare providers, the costs of specific benefits, one's utilization of Medicare's services in the past year, etc. Each type of information likely has a distinct effect on policy preferences.

The data for this analysis include measures of aggregate level knowledge of Medicare. Given the range of information that is possible to know about the Medicare program, it is difficult to assess the validity of the indices used here as representative measures of the entire set of aggregate level Medicare program knowledge. Because the questions that compose the knowledge indices directly ask about Medicare, the indices are likely to be valid measures of what the public knows about these questions.

The knowledge questions used in this study ask about four aspects of the Medicare program: 1) its general purpose, 2) its place in the federal budget, 3) benefits paid by the program, and 4) its financial soundness (Table 6).[37]

Compared with responses to the other questions, the largest number of Americans were able to correctly identify Medicare's purpose. Seventy-seven percent of respondents knew that Medicare is a federal government program and 74 percent knew that Medicare principally serves older Americans. In contrast, only about a third (38 percent) of Americans could correctly identify that all of Medicare is considered part of the federal government budget.[38] When asked about Medicare benefits, Americans were more likely to correctly identify benefits that are offered than to correctly identify benefits that are not offered. Three out of four people knew that Medicare pays doctor bills for older Americans, and less than half knew that Medicare does not pay for long-term nursing care or prescription drugs (49 and 41 percent, respectively). The final, composite question registers the correct response to both questions concerning the financial soundness of the Medicare program. About two-thirds of adults (70 percent) knew that Medicare was in danger of going bankrupt, and about two-thirds of people who answered this question correctly knew that Medicare had been in danger of bankruptcy for a long time. Thus, about one-half of Americans (49 percent) correctly answered both parts of this question.

Table 6: Medicare Program Knowledge Questions, n=1,383

	Percentage who chose category (correct answer is underlined)
1) To the best of your knowledge is Medicare primarily:	
A federal government program,	$\underline{77}$
A state government program,	13
Or a private insurance program?	4
Not sure	6
2) When you hear the word "Medicare" do you think of:	
A program that principally serves poor people of all ages, or	
A program that principally serves the elderly?	22
Not sure	$\underline{74}$
	4
3) Which of the following statements do you think best describes the Medicare program;	
The Medicare program is part of the overall federal government budget,	
The Medicare program is in a separate trust fund independent of the overall federal budget, or	
Part of Medicare is in the overall federal budget and part of it is in a separate trust fund?	$\underline{38}$ / 18
	29
Not sure	14
4) The current Medicare program pays for long-term nursing home care for individuals 65 years of age and older);	
True, or	44
False?	$\underline{49}$
Not sure	6
5) The current Medicare program pays for prescription drugs for individuals 65 years of age and older;	
True, or	54
False?	$\underline{41}$
Not sure	5
6) The current Medicare program pays for doctor bills for individuals 65 years of age and older;	
True, or	$\underline{75}$
False?	22
Not sure	4
7) Part 1: To the best of your knowledge, is Medicare financially sound or is it in danger of going bankrupt;	
Financially sound, or	20
In danger of going bankrupt?	$\underline{70}$
Not sure	10
Part 2: For those who think Medicare is in danger of going bankrupt, is this a new problem for Medicare or has Medicare been in danger of going bankrupt for a long time (n = 928);	
A new problem,	22
Has been in danger for a long time?	$\underline{70}$
Not sure	8

As suggested earlier, it is likely that different types of information are used when a respondent assesses his support for different types of policies. For example, one of the policy questions asks whether or not the government should reduce benefits for seniors to address Medicare's issues or balance the federal budget.[39] The question tells the respondent that Medicare is a government program for seniors, so this information does not have to be retrieved to formulate a response. The most relevant set of information about Medicare needed to make a personal judgment for this question pertains to the benefits offered by Medicare. The person answering the question will likely recall what he knows about the benefits offered, make some assessment of the value of those benefits and the effect of reducing them, and respond. In this case, the respondent's support will likely vary more with the amount of knowledge he has about benefits than with more general knowledge about Medicare.

To test the impact of different sets of knowledge, the effect of two indices is tested throughout this study. The Full Knowledge Index includes all of the seven questions in Table 6.[40] The Benefits Index represents knowledge of Medicare benefits and includes questions 4-6 in Table 6. An assessment of the reliability of these indices suggests that both are adequate measures of the general knowledge and knowledge of benefits asked for in these questions.[41]

Further research is needed to develop more reliable indices that capture various types of knowledge about Medicare and tests the effects over time. The ideal test of the effects of Medicare program knowledge would include several indices, similar to those used in AIDS research, each one focusing on a particular aspect of the Medicare program.[42] Knowledge indices should measure aggregate and specific knowledge, a mix of Medicare program knowledge with other types of political knowledge (to match policy questions that have a political angle), and should be asked on a variety of surveys during different years and different Medicare debates. With more specific and detailed indices we could differentiate the effects of knowledge about financing from knowledge about benefits and discern which knowledge matters in what context. Additionally, asking a series of knowledge questions about the same topic would reduce the likelihood that how the question was asked influenced the respondent's ability to convey his knowledge of Medicare.

Models explaining public opinion concerning public policy typically contain some mix of socio-economic and political variables. In *The Nature and Origins of Mass Opinion*, John Zaller (1992) explains why measures of predisposition are used to explain public opinion. The first step in Zaller's model of opinion formation is the reception of communication, specifically from media. Citizens accept or resist these messages based on a variety of interests, values, and experiences filtered through individual-level, stable traits that regulate the acceptance of political communications. "Because the totality of the communications that one accepts determines one's opinions...predispositions are the critical intervening variable between the communications people encounter in the mass media, on one side, and their statements of political preferences, on the other" (23).[43]

From another perspective, individual policy preferences are determined through a process in which each individual evaluates (implicitly or explicitly) each policy option in terms of individual and societal costs and benefits. The resulting policy choices maximize individual net benefits. Accordingly, variables such as political party and education explain the likelihood of support because they reflect how a Medicare policy option may impact an individual.

For this study the socio-economic and political variables used to predict the likelihood of support for Medicare policy options are limited to questions asked in the survey. The model specification subsequently presented may be thought of as the reduced form model of public opinion corresponding to a more elaborate, unspecified model that, if specified would include all factors that determine public opinion (Bartels 1996). Other factors not included in the model, such as place of employment or measures of social networks, also likely affect policy preferences. For this study, the reduced form captures a sufficient range of mediating factors to demonstrate how information about Medicare can affect policy preferences.

The model used to explain Medicare policy preferences for this analysis follows.[44] Tables A1-A2 in the Appendix for Chapter Two describe each variable in more detail. [45]

Medicare Policy Preferences	=	Age	+	Age*Knowledge
		Party	+	Party*Knowledge
		Ideology	+	Ideology*Knowledge
		Education	+	Education*Knowledge
		Race	+	Race*Knowledge
		Income	+	Income*Knowledge
		Sex	+	Sex*Knowledge

The Medicare policy options used as dependent variables in this study ask respondents for their support for reform options prominent during debates about Medicare occurring at the time of the survey (Tables 7-8).[46,47]

Two of the policy questions ask about support for changes that would have altered the financing mechanism for Medicare from the current predominantly fee-for-service financing to a voucher system or private managed care plans. The remaining four policy options left the current Medicare system intact. One of these proposals relied on increased financial support from the public to address Medicare's issues and two of the three remaining proposals placed the cost of reform on Medicare beneficiaries.

Based on these six reform options, Americans were most supportive of the status quo at the time of this survey. Only one option, the proposal to enroll Medicare beneficiaries in managed care plans did not have a majority of support for not changing Medicare. The proportion of Americans supportive of managed care for Medicare recipients (49 percent) does not differ statistically from the proportion of respondents who opposed this proposal (48 percent). In comparison, only 36 percent of Americans preferred to change Medicare to a voucher system to address its financing issues and 41 percent would have changed the age of eligibility for Medicare from 65 to 67 in the year 2000.

Similarly, the public was not supportive of proposals to raise the cost of Medicare for beneficiaries. Sixty-five percent of Americans thought that the government should not raise monthly premiums for beneficiaries. Additionally, an overwhelming majority of Americans (80 percent) thought that the government should not reduce benefits to Medicare recipients to either save Medicare from bankruptcy or balance the federal budget. Finally, twenty-nine percent of Americans supported raising payroll taxes to address Medicare's problems.

Table 7: Descriptive Statistics for Medicare Policy Questions, n = 1,383

Dependent Variables	% of respondents
Some people have suggested the following proposal as a way to keep Medicare from going bankrupt/to reduce future Medicare spending in order to balance the budget and avoid raising taxes. Under this proposal, Medicare would no longer provide people directly with a health insurance policy. Instead, Medicare would give people a check or voucher for a fixed amount each year and you would buy your own health insurance policy. Would you prefer to...	
Keep the current system	62
Receive a check or voucher	36
Not sure	2

Table 8: Descriptive statistics for Medicare Policy Questions, n = 1,383

Dependent Variables	% favor	% oppose	% not sure
I am going to read you a list of some ways to keep Medicare from going bankrupt/to reduce future Medicare spending in order to balance the budget and avoid raising taxes. For each, please tell me if you would favor or oppose such a proposal? The age at which people become eligible for Medicare should be raised from age 65 to age67 after the year 2000	41	57	1
Do you favor or oppose the following proposal: Instead of most Medicare recipients being enrolled in the traditional fee-for-service Medicare program, most Medicare recipients would be enrolled in private managed care plans. These managed care plans might provide enrollees with additional benefits for no more money, but enrollees would have less choice of doctors and hospitals when seeking care.	49	48	3
Keeping in mind the financial problems that might cause Medicare to go bankrupt/In thinking about balancing the federal budget, which of the following do you think the government should do?	% should	% should not	% not sure
Reduce benefits to senior	18	80	2
Raise payroll taxes	29	68	3
Raise the monthly premiums for all Medicare recipients	32	65	3

Interest groups concerned about whether or not to educate the public during policy debates are particularly interested in understanding the impact of information on segments of the population that they may target. Additionally, information is expected to have a different impact on different segments of the population according to their interest or stake in a particular policy option. The following descriptions provide a basis for understanding how many people within each segment of the population could shift from being poorly informed to being well informed and how the base differs by general or benefits information.

Beginning with the Full Index, I define a high level of knowledge about Medicare as five or more of seven possible correct answers.[48] By this definition, 38 percent of Americans have a high level and a majority of adults (62 percent) have a low level of Medicare knowledge. The average level of knowledge is four and three-fourths of the population (76 percent) have index scores of three to five.

Figure 10 shows that within the large majority of groups that can divide the public, the majority of adults are poorly informed about the Full Index of Medicare knowledge. A probit analysis of the likelihood of being well informed indicates which characteristics predict the likelihood of being well informed. Adults 65 years of age or older, with income of $25,000 or more, or with a college degree/post graduate education are more likely to be informed than adults 49 years of age or younger, with less than $25,000 in income, and with the equivalent of a high school degree, respectively. Additionally, African-American adults are less likely than are white Americans to be well informed.

Figure 10: Mix of Poorly and Well Informed Among Segments of the Population (Full Index)

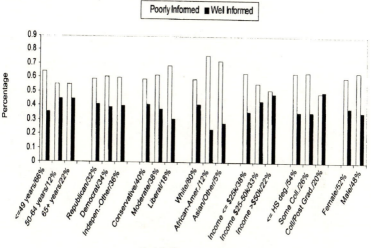

Population Characteristics/% of pop.

For the Benefits Index of questions about Medicare, people are well informed if they answer two of the three questions correctly. By this definition, 56 percent of Americans are well informed and 44 percent are poorly informed. The average score for this index is 1.64. While the questions of this index are more specific, the lower number of correct responses needed to be considered well informed may indicate a higher likelihood of guessing a correct answer that would shift you from being poorly informed to well informed. While a majority of all but one segment of the population is considered well informed, a considerable minority in each case could know more about Medicare benefits.

Interestingly, the higher level of knowledge indicated by the Benefits Index when compared with the Full Index is demonstrated consistently across segments of the population (Figure 11). However, only two specific characteristics of the population divided by the Benefits Index significantly predict the likelihood of being informed. Not surprisingly, Medicare recipients are significantly more likely to be well informed about their benefits than are Americans 49 years or younger. Additionally, people who are

Asian or belong to other ethnic groups are less likely than are white Americans to be well informed about Medicare benefits.

Figure 11: Mix of Poorly and Well Informed Among Segments of the Population (Specific Index)

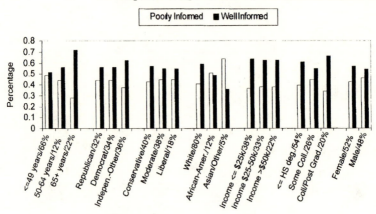

Population Characteristics/% of pop.

ANALYTICAL RESULTS

The first hypothesis predicts that as an independent variable knowledge will not have a significant effect on the likelihood of support for Medicare policy. To test this assertion, each policy option was regressed on socio-economic and political variables and each of the two Knowledge Indices. The Indices are coded 1 for well informed Americans and 0 for poorly informed Americans, as previously defined.

The Full Knowledge variable had no independent effect on the likelihood of support for five of the six policies analyzed (Table 9) shows the change in the likelihood of support caused by being well informed; Tables A3-A14 in the Appendix for Chapter Two show parameter estimates with standard errors).[49] When controlling for socio-political variables, well informed Americans' likelihood of support for these policies did not differ significantly from poorly informed Americans' likelihood of support. Being more knowledgeable did affect the predicted probability of support for favoring an increase in premiums paid by Medicare recipients (Table 9). Compared with being poorly informed about the Full Index, being knowledgeable decreased the predicted probability of support by 0.08.[50] Expressed differently, holding the public's characteristics as they were in 1995, educating them about the Full Index of Medicare information would have decreased support for an increase in premiums by eight percentage points.

Table 9: The Effect of Knowledge on the Predicted Probability of Support for Medicare Policy Options

Medicare Policy Option	DY/Dx of the Full Index	DY/Dx of the Specific Index
Voucher system	0.06	-0.02
Managed care	0.05	-0.02
Increasing the payroll tax	0.03	0.00
Changing the age of eligibility	0.04	-0.06
Decreasing benefits for beneficiaries	-0.03	-0.05*
Increasing premiums for beneficiaries	-0.08*	-0.09*

Notes: 1) Models calculated using robust standard errors. 2) DY/Dx designates how much the independent variable being true changes the outcome probability over that of the independent variable being false. 3) * p <= 0.05.

The Benefits Index affected the level of support for two of the six policies. *Ceteris paribus*, educating the public with information about Medicare's benefits would have decreased the predicted probability of support for increasing premiums by 0.09. In a similar comparison, increasing knowledge about Medicare benefits would have decreased support for decreasing benefits by five percentage points.

Generally, whether a person was knowledgeable about Medicare was not an independent predictor of support for these policies. Of the 12 tests, nine supported the first hypothesis. However, for the Benefits Index, one third of the models did not support the first hypothesis and showed independent effects for knowledge.

When the Indices did predict support, these variables seemed to be capturing a characteristic of the public not incorporated in the other determinants, such as the role of factual information or engagement. Adding the knowledge variables to the models for predicting support for increasing premiums or decreasing benefits did not change significantly the effect of any of the other determinants of support (Tables A3-A14 in the Appendix for Chapter Two).

Educating the general public about Medicare could matter for a few, select policy options. In this case, options that directly affect costs or benefits for current beneficiaries are affected by how much people know about Medicare. Considering the already low levels of support for either of these options, the magnitude of the changes are notable. Finally, for this model changing the level of knowledge would not have shifted the position of the majority of the public.

The previous analysis assumes that knowledge would have the same effect across all segments of the population. According to these results and theory previously discussed, the impact of knowledge likely occurs via other determinants of Medicare policy. Recalling a previous example, the effect of income on the likelihood of support for increasing the age of eligibility for the Medicare program in a well informed population may differ significantly from its effect in a poorly informed public. Well informed citizens, regardless of income, may balance short-term and long-term, individual and societal costs associated with this proposal against a comparable range of benefits and decide to support the change. In contrast, poorly informed Americans may be more likely to only consider the short-term, individual monetary costs or benefits that correlate with income. The result would be a difference in the effect of income between the two knowledge groups.

Hypothesis two contends that information affects the likelihood of support for Medicare policy proposals via calculations of how policies will affect segments of the population. For segments of the population affected by a proposed change in Medicare policy, more information should significantly change the likelihood of support.

The differential effect of knowledge on the other determinants of support for Medicare policy is demonstrated by adding an interaction term to the original models. Here, the dummy variable for knowledge is multiplied by the dummy variable for each determinant. The resulting coefficients (shown in the second and fifth columns of Tables 15-20 in the Appendix for Chapter Two) reveal the difference in the effect of each variable for more knowledgeable people compared with less knowledgeable people.[51] Tables 10-11 highlight the changes in the likelihood of support contributed to this interaction effect.

Table 10: The Change in the Predicted Probability of Support Caused by Changing Each Group From Poorly Informed to Well Informed (DY/Dx for the Interaction Term) – Full Index

	Voucher	HMO, etc.	Increase Payroll Tax	Change Age Eligibility	< Benefit $	> Premiums
Age 18-49 (ref)						
Age 50- 64	0.16	-0.03	-0.06	0.04	0.14	-0.06
Age 65+	0.04	-0.01	0.00	0.05	0.18*	0.14
Republican Party (ref)						
Democrat	0.01	0.03	0.07	0.10	-0.03	-0.08
Independent/Other	0.06	-0.04	0.06	0.07	0.06	-0.13
Conservative ideology(ref)						
Moderate	-0.04	0.03	-0.02	-0.02	-0.01	0.01
Liberal	-0.08	-0.06	-0.03	-0.12	0.00	-0.01
White Race (ref)						
African-American	0.16	-0.07	-0.15	-0.16	0.08	-0.05
Asian/other	0.23	0.01	-0.03	-0.10	-0.03	0.04
Income < = $25,000 (ref)						
Income $25,001- $50,000	-0.07	0.02	0.06	-0.01	-0.01	-0.04
Income > = $50,001	0.05	-0.12	-0.06	0.04	0.02	-0.01
H.S. deg./equiv. or less (ref)						
Some college	-0.12	-0.05	-0.06	0.06	0.20*	-0.02
College/post. graduate deg.	-0.10	-0.00	-0.07	-0.06	0.12	0.00
Female (ref)						
Male	0.07	-0.04	0.01	0.04	0.08	0.12

Notes: 1) Model calculated using robust standard errors. 2) The interaction term is the Knowledge Index (coded 0,1) multiplied by each independent variable (coded 0,1). 3) DY/Dx designates how much the independent variable being true changes the outcome probability over that of the independent variable being false. 4) * p <= 0.05.

Table 11: The Change in the Predicted Probability of Support Caused by Changing Each Group
From Poorly Informed to Well Informed (DY/Dx for the Interaction Term) – Benefits Index

	Voucher	HMO, etc.	Increase Payroll Tax	Change Age Eligibility	< Benefit $	> Premiums
Age 18-49 (ref)						
Age 50- 64	0.00	0.08	0.01	0.00	0.04	-0.01
Age 65+	-0.11	-0.17*	-0.10	-0.06	-0.02	0.09
Republican Party (ref)						
Democrat	0.15	0.05	0.14	0.07	-0.02	0.03
Independent/Other	0.15	0.02	-0.01	0.07	0.07	0.07
Conservative ideology(ref)						
Moderate	-0.14*	-0.04	-0.04	0.03	-0.03	0.02
Liberal	-0.05	-0.10	-0.18*	-0.14	-0.06	-0.06
White Race (ref)						
African-American	0.00	0.06	-0.03	-0.21*	-0.12	-0.11
Asian/other	0.32*	0.09	0.05	0.09	-0.04	0.13
Income < = $25,000 (ref)						
Income $25,001- $50,000	0.06	0.05	0.10	0.03	-0.06	-0.05
Income > = $50,001	0.02	-0.07	-0.01	0.06	-0.08	-0.00
H.S. deg./equiv. or less (ref)						
Some college	-0.11	-0.08	0.01	0.05	0.15*	-0.03
College/post. graduate deg.	-0.10	0.03	0.20*	0.15	0.13	0.07
Female (ref)						
Male	-0.14*	-0.04	0.07	-0.05	0.00	0.06

Notes: 1) Model calculated using robust standard errors. 2) The interaction term is the Knowledge Index (coded 0,1) multiplied by each independent variable (coded 0,1). 3) DY/Dx designates how much the independent variable being true changes the outcome probability over that of the independent variable being false. 4) * p <= 0.05.

The Full Index provided scant support for the second hypothesis (Table 10). Of the 19 combinations of segments of the population and policy options where information was predicted to have a significant effect, only one information effect was significant. Being 65 years of age or more had a 0.18 greater impact on the predicted probability of support for reducing benefits for Americans well informed about the Full Index than on the support of poorly informed Americans. Expressed differently, well informed older Americans are more likely than poorly informed older Americans to support a decrease in Medicare benefits.

While this specific effect was not predicted by the hypothesis, having some college education has a 0.20 greater impact on the likelihood of support for decreasing benefits for well informed adults than for poorly informed adults. Expressed differently, well informed people with some college education are more likely than poorly informed people with some college education to support decreasing Medicare benefits.

The results for the Benefits Index support hypotheses two and three (which predicts more effects for this index), but not as expected. Of the 19 expected significant effects for the Benefits Index, only three materialized (Table 11). While this number is more than for the Full Index, the number is not a sizable portion of the number of effects expected.

Tables 11 demonstrates how assuming that knowledge effects are the same for all types of people (presented earlier) hides information effects. For example, while knowledge as an independent variable did not affect the likelihood of support for favoring an increase in the payroll tax, it does affect how other variables impact support for this option (Table 11). A liberal person who is well informed about Medicare's benefits is 18 percentage points less supportive than is a poorly informed liberal person of an increase in the payroll tax to support Medicare. Likewise, a college graduate who is well informed about Medicare's benefits is 20 percentage points more supportive than is a poorly informed college graduate of increasing the payroll tax to support Medicare. Similarly, the Benefits Index also affected the level of support for a voucher system for Medicare. Well informed people with moderate ideology and well informed men were less likely to support a voucher system than their poorly informed counterparts.[52]

In the first part of these results, Medicare knowledge affected the likelihood of support for up to two of the six policies examined in this study. For both policies, increasing the level of knowledge from poorly informed to well informed would have decreased support for the proposed changes to Medicare financing. One implication of these findings is that organizations interested in shifting public opinion about the options via education could blanket the public with information and see significant effects.

The second part of these results demonstrates that for some Medicare policies knowledge can impact support via an interaction with other determinants of policy preferences. This interaction effect provides another level of insight into the role of Medicare knowledge and also reveals substantial effects.

For example, Americans 65 years of age and older (older Americans) are relatively easy to provide with information about Medicare benefits because a sizable portion of them belong to AARP or receive information from the Health Care Financing Administration, the organization that administers Medicare. A campaign at the time of this survey to increase the level of knowledge of poorly informed older Americans (55 percent of older Americans) could have increased their level of support for reducing benefits to address Medicare's issues by 18 percentage points. Knowing the effect of knowledge would have prevented AARP from wasting resources on members who are 50-64 years old and provided a mechanism with which they could influence support among their members for an option that was untenable at the time and may be unavoidable in the near future. Although successful efforts to further educate poorly informed older Americans about Medicare benefits would have shifted support for raising benefits for only 12 percent of the population, a major shift in the position of Medicare beneficiaries would have commanded attention and likely influenced the political activity of this group and other representatives of older Americans.

The general explanation for why some groups are affected by the level of information and others are not concerns the nature of the particular policy in question. Some groups more easily identify with particular issues; or, the salience of the issue may be enhanced for some people by political rhetoric crafted to appeal to particular groups (Bartels 1996). For example, people with liberal ideology may identify an increase in the payroll tax as a regressive tax that would inordinately affect people with low incomes. Thus, having more knowledge about Medicare may enable the person to more closely link this option with their ideological position and decrease their level of support (Table 11).

Along with demonstrating information effects for segments of the population, this study also supports the idea that different types of information about Medicare have different effects (the third hypothesis). Among the six policies examined, support for decreasing benefits was the only policy that the Full Index affected via other determinants of Medicare policy. In contrast, support for decreasing benefits was the only variable that the Benefits Index did not affect via at least one interaction. Additionally, the effect of the Benefits Index varies across the different policy options.[53]

For researchers interested in Medicare policy outcomes, the ultimate test of information effects is to show how knowledge affects the overall predicted probability of support.[54] Tables 12-13 compare the predicted probability of support with the current distribution of knowledge in the public with the predicted probability of support for a well informed public with the same characteristics.[55] The results show shifts in support that could occur if all people poorly informed about Medicare were well informed about Medicare.

For five of the six policies, having a well informed public changes support for these policy options slightly, but significantly, which supports the first hypothesis. For example, informing the public about the Full Index increases the predicted probability of support for a voucher system by 0.03 (Table 12). The largest shift in predicted support due to educating the public with general information about Medicare, 0.03, occurs for three of the six policies.

Similarly, for the Benefits Index, educating the public had a significant effect on the predicted probability of support for five of the six policies (Table 13). The largest impact for the Benefits Index affected the willingness to increase premiums to address Medicare's issues. Informing the public about Medicare benefits decreased the predicted probability of support for increased premiums by 0.03.

Comparing the results in Table 12 with the results in Table 13 supports hypothesis three, which claims a difference in effects for the two knowledge indices. Fully educating the public about the Full Index or the Benefits Index would affect differently the predicted probability of support for Medicare policy options. For example, for four of the six policies, educating the public with the general information increases the predicted probability of support. When using the Benefits Index to calculate support, educating the public decreases support for five of the six policies.

Because support for Medicare policy tends to be lopsided and a sizable minority of the public is well informed about Medicare, the shift in support that would occur if all of the public were well informed with either set of knowledge would not shift the majority. A possible exception concerns changing the age of eligibility for Medicare. Fully educating the public with the Full Index would shift American's support for changing the age of eligibility for Medicare from 65 to 67 after the year 2000 from 49 percent to 51 percent (Table 12).

Table 12: Changes in Predicted Probability of Support for Medicare Policy Options Due to Changes in the Level of Full Knowledge about Medicare

Medicare Policy Option	Predicted Probability of Y=1 for the Public (SE)	Predicted Probability of Y=1 for a "Well- Informed" Public (SE)	Difference
Full Knowledge Index Willingness to Favor A Voucher System for Medicare	0.316 0.004	0.346 0.005	0.030* 0.002
Willingness to Favor Moving Beneficiaries from Fee-for-Service to Managed Care	0.463 0.005	0.487 0.004	0.024* 0.002
Willingness to Favor an Increase in the Payroll Tax to Address Medicare's Issues	0.314 0.002	0.326 0.003	0.012* 0.002
Willingness to Favor Increasing the Age of Eligibility from 65 to 67 in the Year 2000 to Address Medicare's Issues	0.488 0.004	0.514 0.004	0.026* 0.002
Willingness to Favor a Reduction in Benefits to Medicare Recipients to Address Medicare's Issues	0.188 0.003	0.187 0.003	-0.001 0.002
Willingness to Favor an Increase in Premiums to Address Medicare's Issues	0.379 0.003	0.350 0.004	-0.028* 0.002

*p <= 0.05

Table 13: Changes in Predicted Probability of Support for Medicare Policy Options Due to Changes in the Level of Medicare Benefits Knowledge

Medicare Policy Option	Predicted Probability of Y=1 for the Public (SE)	Predicted Probability of Y=1 for a "Well- Informed" Public (SE)	Difference
Full Knowledge Index Willingness to Favor A Voucher System for Medicare	0.316 0.005	0.303 0.004	-0.013* 0.002
Willingness to Favor Moving Beneficiaries from Fee-for-Service to Managed Care	0.462 0.005	0.450 0.005	-0.011* 0.002
Willingness to Favor an Increase in the Payroll Tax to Address Medicare's Issues	0.315 0.003	0.319 0.003	0.004* 0.002
Willingness to Favor Increasing the Age of Eligibility from 65 to 67 in the Year 2000 to Address Medicare's Issues	0.491 0.004	0.473 0.005	-0.018* 0.002
Willingness to Favor a Reduction in Benefits to Medicare Recipients to Address Medicare's Issues	0.187 0.003	0.171 0.002	-0.016* 0.002
Willingness to Favor an Increase in Premiums to Address Medicare's Issues	0.381 0.003	0.354 0.004	-0.027* 0.002

*$p <= 0.05$

DISCUSSION/IMPLICATIONS

This study enhances our understanding of information effects during public policy debates, which is a form of political contest. The impact of knowledge on Medicare reform proposals is used to establish the existence of these effects and to inform groups or policy experts interested in investing in efforts to educate the public about Medicare policy.

The results suggest that educating the public with general or benefits information about Medicare could slightly shift policy preferences. Additionally, these effects on support evidently would occur by targeting particular groups with a particular set of information. Knowledge of Medicare benefits is shown to have sizable interaction effects that could shift support among liberals, older Americans or college graduates depending on the policy option.

In addition to the information effects demonstrated here, this study suggests that different types of policy-related information can have different effects on policy preferences. Both the size of the effect and which groups are affected varies by Medicare policy.

These findings suggest that broad based education campaigns concerning Medicare, especially campaigns conveyed via media, are not the most effective way to instigate large shifts in the public's support for a broad range of Medicare policy proposals. Specific aggregate level information produced more effects than general Medicare information and media campaigns are better suited for general bits of information that can be understood in very small amounts of time. Additionally, media cannot target audience members with particular sets of information to take advantage of the interaction effects shown.

Further research using other indices, as previously discussed, would provide a more comprehensive understanding of how the effects vary by information and policy type. Additionally, a more objective, comprehensive analysis of how each segment of the population would likely be affected by particular Medicare policy options would also further enhance our understanding of the patterns of effects. Finally, predictions that incorporate the remaining factors represented by the knowledge index (e.g., engagement and cognitive ability) would also expand insights into the results.

The information effects demonstrated with Medicare knowledge and policy options could be more dramatic with a health issue decided in the political arena of which the public is less well informed or is more evenly divided in their support. Support for new health policy issues, such as cloning, or issues that are more complex, such as health policy reform, likely vary more with changes to levels of knowledge about each issue.

Notes

[24] The specific information that influences the decisions of elected officials has been difficult to establish empirically. Kingdon (1981,1995) provides a model of policymaking that incorporates both sets of information. Additionally, anecdotal evidence from political and policy consultants, such as Robert J. Blendon, and accounts of health policy debates, such as *The System: The American Way of Politics at the Breaking Point* by Hanes Johnson and David Broder, suggest that this assertion is valid.

[25] See Lodge and McGraw (1996) for a more comprehensive understanding of the information-processing approach to studying political judgment.

[26] Zaller defines the following key concepts for his model: A consideration is any reason that may induce an individual to decide a political issue one way or another. Persuasive messages are arguments or images providing reasons for taking a position or point of view. Once accepted, they become considerations. Cueing messages consist of contextual information about ideology or the partisan implications of a persuasive message. Cueing messages enable citizens to perceive relationships between the persuasive messages they receive and their political predispositions that permits them to respond critically to the persuasive messages.

[27] Sniderman. Brody, & Tetlock's use of education as a proxy for political sophistication, while understandable given the constraints of most public opinion surveys and other data, does not clearly differentiate between the effects of each component of political sophistication.

[28] For Lupia, the level of knowledge refers to the number of correct responses to questions concerning characteristics of ballot initiatives. How "well informed" is defined varies. Generally, the well informed can answer correctly a majority of factual questions about politics (which vary by analysis), political actors, or public policy. Normative discussions concerning what people should know, specifically, about the political system or how well they should know this information are rare.

[29] See the following sources for the evolution of debate among political scientists concerning the "Nature of Belief Systems in Mass Publics" (title by Converse 1964) and specifically, the role of political knowledge: Lazarsfeld, Berelson, and Gaudet 1944; Converse 1964; For a revisionist view of previous frameworks refer to: Nie, Verba, and Petrocik 1976; Conover and Feldman 1981; Sullivan, Piereson, Marcus 1978; For the rationality of public opinion at the aggregate level refer to: Stimson 1991; and Page and Shapiro 1992); For the latest empirical evidence reviewing

what voters know about politics refer to: Luskin 1987; Smith 1989;
Delli Carpini and Keeter 1996.

[30] Across all of these studies differences between highly knowledgeable
and less knowledgeable people vary according to the content and mix of
persuasive message, exposure to political messages, the complexity of the
political context, or the methods used to capture these variables.
Additionally, numerous studies of how political knowledge mediates the
impact of media or the role of information in the evaluation of candidates
or presidential performance use various combinations of factors which
combined are called political sophistication or attentiveness. These factors
include factual knowledge, reported interest in a political contest, and
exposure to news. The resulting evidence for the effect of factual knowledge on political attitudes and behavior is mixed. See Krosnick and
Brannon (1993) for a discussion of the mix of empirical evidence of the
moderating role of political expertise. See Zaller (1996) for evidence of
why and how the operationalization of knowledge as an indicator of the
reception of persuasive political messages via mass media matters. More
indirectly, Iyengar and Kinder (1987) use knowledge of a policy problem
to predict ratings of the importance of the problem as a way to assess the
impact of media on the public's policy agenda. Problem expertise was one
indicator of seven measures of political involvement which, along with
education and party identification, were used to predict policy importance. For their analysis, problem expertise did not have an independent
effect on the ratings which suggested that the effect of television news on
the public's agenda did not depend on problem expertise.

[31] Here, each respondent's level of political knowledge is evaluated and
reported by interviewers for the American National Election Studies.

[32] Engagement refers to the idea that a person interested in the debate
may be more likely to recall factual information because they have
engaged in conversations with friends that have reinforced what they had
previously heard.

[33] All analyses are performed on weighted data, unless otherwise noted.
Although the samples were drawn to emulate a nationally representative
sample, random fluctuations can cause the sample to not match exactly
the demographic composition of the national, adult population. A weight
is assigned to each observation to assure that the sample match more pre-
cisely the population. For these data, weights were applied to adjust the
distribution of education and age by race by sex to match the March 1994
CPS figures (Brodie 1995, 139). The weights have the following characteristics: mean = 0.99999, standard deviation = 0.65, minimum = 0.19,

maximum = 3.18, 11 weights >= 3, 100 weights >= 2, 775 weights >= 1, and 515 weights >= 0.5.

[34] According to a conversation with Paul McGee on April 23, 1998, an expert on sampling at Louis Harris Associates, Inc., the stratification is used to ensure that replacements are from the same geographical region. The replacements are generated randomly and continue until the target sample size is reached.

[35] According to a conversation with Paul McGee on April 23, 1998, the response rate was 48 percent.

[36] McGraw and Pinney (1990) show that general and domain-specific political expertise have distinct and theoretically meaningful consequences for political cognition. These categories apply their demarcation between types of expertise to knowledge of particular issue.

[37] Blendon et al. (1995) provide an excellent analysis of what people knew about the Medicare program in 1995.

[38] "Americans" refers to the adults interviewed for this survey. Because this is a sample subject to error, the adults surveyed may not represent all Americans. However, based on the sampling procedures, the sample size, and the quality of the instrument (all designed to reduce sources of error), I am confident that the responses are a reasonable representation of the preferences of the American public in the coterminous United States. Additionally, there may have been some confusion about the correct response given the wording of this question. The question asks whether or not Medicare is part of the federal government budget, in a trust fund separate from the federal budget, or a mix of both options. In fact, revenues for Part A of Medicare (which pays for hospital care) go through what the government calls a "trust fund" that, along with financing for other services, is included in the federal budget (Moon 1997).

[39] Politicians justified the reform proposals suggested at the time of the survey with a variety of reasons. To test how the purpose for the proposed change affected the responses, the sample was split into two groups with similar demographic characteristics and each group was asked a series of policy questions framed with one of two explanations. Analysis of the results showed no statistical difference in the level of support for each option between these two groups.

[40] Each knowledge question was coded 1 if the respondent answered correctly and 0 if the respondent answered incorrectly or "not sure." Thus, the poorly informed are people who did not give a correct answer. The index is a score ranging from 0-7 that represents the number of questions each person answered correctly. The Benefits Index is similarly coded.

[41] The reliability coefficient for the Full Index is 0.62 and for the Benefits Index is 0.62. Chronbach's alpha assesses how well the indices correlate with the factor that is being measured which, in this case, is a range of knowledge about the Medicare program. It is possible that the reliability of the Full Index is mostly determined by the specific questions. Analyses using the two indices suggest that the Full Index has a different effect than the Benefits Index. Additionally, a third index including questions 1-3 was also tested for reliability. This index was not included because the three questions did not capture similar concepts (alpha = 0.17).

[42] For examples see Nicholas 1996; VanLandingham 1997; Imperato 1996; Zagumny 1995; and Furnham 1992.

[43] Zaller describes the sources of political predispositions as "...in part a distillation of a person's lifetime experiences, including childhood socialization and direct involvement with the raw ingredients of policy issues, such as earning a living, paying taxes, racial (or sexual) discrimination, and so forth. Predispositions also partly depend on social and economic location and, probably at least as strongly, on inherited or acquired personality factors and tastes." (23)

[44] This model assumes a linear relationship in the interactions between knowledge and the remaining variables (discussed subsequently). Theory suggests that nonlinear forms may be more representative of these relationships (Bartels 1996). Further expansion of this study would determine the sensitivity of the results to the functional form of the model.

[45] An analysis of the correlation between these variables indicates low levels of collinearity. The highest correlation coefficient was 0.41 and describes the correlation between income and education. I include income in the final regressions because excluding this variable did not significantly affect the resulting analyses and maximizes the amount of information supporting the results.

[46] For the dependent variables, don't know/not sure responses were coded as missing because this analysis focuses on the impact of knowledge on expressed opinions. The tables of descriptive information show the percentage of values in these categories to not exceed three percent of any question. Additionally, the same categories were coded as missing for the independent variables. Except for income, the percentages of missing for the independent variables were also negligible. The largest category of missing data was for income. Income remained unreported for 70 respondents. In order to take advantage of the other information available from these observations in the regression analyses, the mean income for respondents with equivalent age and education was used as the income for the

missing values. Where education was not available the mean for age was used. Regression results including and excluding these observations were compared and none of the effects changed significantly (Brodie 1995).

[47] The survey contains 21 policy options that could have been included in this analysis. To facilitate the analysis I chose seven options that represent the range of proposals discussed during the policy debates about Medicare in 1995. A copy of the survey instrument may be viewed upon request.

[48] The demarcation between low and high levels of knowledge is somewhat arbitrary. I chose the 75th percentile to divide people well informed about Medicare from their counterparts. The 75th percentile separation groups people with medium levels of Medicare program knowledge with people with low levels of knowledge for both indices.

[49] The level of significance is 0.05.

[50] DY/Dx represents the difference in the likelihood of support for a particular category of people and its reference category.

[51] The analytical methods for this study are inspired by methods designed to capture the effect of information in presidential elections (Bartels 1996).

[52] The Benefits Index also affected the impact of the Asian/other racial category. This effect is difficult to interpret because of the heterogeneity of the groups that it represents and the small number of people in this category. This analysis focuses on the effect of information on the two policies for which knowledge had an independent effect and two examples for which knowledge had significant effects. The Appendix contains the regressions for the remaining policy options.

[53] As Bartels (1996) notes, one could argue that the patterns revealed by dividing the public by level of knowledge could be attributed to the effect of unmeasured characteristics differentiating the well-informed from the less well-informed in a particular demographic category. "Whatever those unmeasured factors are, they must (1) be strongly correlated with differences in (knowledge about Medicare, and in this case with each specific index differently), (2) *not* be *consequences* of differences in political information, and (3) operate distinctly in a particular demographic group..." (215)

[54] The predicted probabilities are calculated using STATA. Incorporated into these calculations is the uncertainty around the parameter estimates. One method for narrowing this uncertainty is to simulate thousands of regressions from similar samples that, in total, would generate parameter estimates that would more closely reflect the value of the coefficients for the population. The parameters calculated in this way would then be used

to calculate predicted probabilities that more closely reflect the predicted probabilities for the population.

[55] The predicted probability of support for the public was calculated by STATA from the full model including the knowledge variables. A separate model was calculated which provided a parameter estimate for each independent variable for well informed Americans and for poorly informed Americans. The predicted probability for the "well informed" public was calculated by applying the parameter estimates for the well informed to the full population.

CHAPTER THREE

Political Participation

Since the passage of Medicare and the Older Americans Act in 1965, the political preferences, voting behavior, and political activity of younger Americans have been compared to the same attitudes and behaviors of older Americans. While the popular press and elected officials often behave as if a galvanized group of "greedy geezers" could topple elected officials who threaten their interests, more sophisticated analyses suggest a complex picture.

Rosenstone and Hansen's analysis (1993) of political activity during presidential elections from 1956-1988 shows that during this period, age had an independent effect on the likelihood of voting, volunteering for a political party, persuading others to vote in a particular way, and contributing to a political party. Consistent with the perception in the popular press, age is a strong determinant of whether a person is likely to participate in politics.

However, because citizens engage in political activity in large part to convey to politicians their policy preferences, a logical, subsequent question is, "Does age predict policy positions or votes?" Peterson and Somit (1994) think not. Based on prior research, they argue that political influence has three prerequisites, two of which are commanded by older Americans.[56] According to Peterson and Somit: "The elderly are, and will be increasingly, very numerous; they are assiduous voters, and should be even more so in the future; but, with possible rare exceptions, it is a serious error to view them as a cohesive voting bloc with a clear sense of self-interest, one which consistently and frequently sets them apart from other groups in our society" (175).

Despite the lack of analytical evidence of a consistent voting bloc of older Americans, a more rigorous comparison between the political activity of older and younger Americans is warranted in order to understand how certain health issues could affect electoral outcomes. The growing percentage of older Americans in the population and their demands for health services ensure that health issues that affect them especially, such as nursing home care or funding for assistive technology, will become an increasingly large focus of attention for the federal government. As their issues become even more prominent, older Americans should be more motivated to protect an increasing stake in government services and policies by influencing political decisions. Further analysis of the political participation of older Americans will enable us to understand the political implications of an older population combined with political agendas more laden with issues that they care about.

This study expands our understanding of age as a predictor of political activity by examining how the political participation and mobilization of older Americans have varied across recent presidential elections. The premise of this analysis is that older Americans will attempt to influence presidential elections at different rates when issues, like Medicare, in which older Americans have a sizable and unique stake emerge on the political agenda. This premise is examined by empirically testing the following questions: Are older Americans even more over-represented among voters or people who try to persuade others to vote for a particular candidate or party when Medicare is an issue? What is the impact of age on the likelihood of voting or persuading one to vote a particular way when Medicare is a campaign issue? Will political parties attempt to mobilize the elderly differently when issues like Medicare/Social Security provide further incentive for political participation? Finally, is the impact of age on the likelihood of participation or mobilization sensitive to how one defines "older Americans"?

The following sections define "political participation" and "older Americans." The next section contains a review of literature on the general effect of age on political activity and is followed by explanations of the models used for this study. Next, is a documentation of the role of Medicare in the 1996 presidential election as compared with 1988 and 1992 that supports the hypotheses that follow. Finally, a description of the data and methods is followed by a discussion of results and implications.

DEFINING "POLITICAL PARTICIPATION" AND "OLDER AMERICANS"

Verba, Schlozman, and Brady (1995) define political participation as "...activity that has the intent or effect of influencing government action—either directly by affecting the making or implementation of public policy or indirectly by influencing the selection of people who influence those policies" (38). Activities, such as volunteering to work for a campaign, contributing money to a campaign, attending rallies, voting, grass-roots lobbying, and working for an advocacy organization, enable Americans, to directly express their preferences for candidates, political parties, and policies. These mechanisms also transfer resources from participants to candidates and enable candidates to run television ads, collect and disseminate information, conduct polls, hire consultants, and undertake other activities needed for political discourse, persuasion, and vote getting.

Another, more indirect, form of political activity of interest to researchers is the act of attempting to persuade others to vote for a particular party or candidate.[57] Attempting to persuade a friend or family member to vote for a particular party or candidate conveys an explicit message about the persuaders political preferences and the rate of this activity among adults varies more than reported voter turnout across elections.

Testing hypotheses concerning the effect of age in three presidential elections requires the selection of political activities that involved a large enough number of activists to make meaningful statistical comparisons. Based on the various modes of participation captured by the National Elections Studies the foci of this study are two different forms of political activity in which a considerable number of people engage each year—reported voter turnout and attempts to persuade others.

An important question that researchers interested in the behavior of older Americans must address is, How should we define 'older Americans'? One response defines older Americans as being 65 years of age and older based on the retirement age set by the Social Security Act of 1935 and later set as the age for receiving Medicare benefits.

The heterogeneous mix of ages, physical conditions, and assessments of health within the population of older adults causes many researchers to use multiple age categories to compare the behavior of older Americans with that of younger Americans and to compare behaviors of older people across categories. The "standard" terminology includes the young-old (65-74 years), the old-old (75-84 years), and the oldest-old (85 years and more) (Peterson and Somit 1994). The able-elderly (older people in good health) are another group of interest to researchers who study the activities of older Americans (Hudson 1987).

This analysis views older Americans as a politically active and visible group during presidential elections. The results focus on comparisons around 65 years of age as the chronological cutoff that reflects a current stake in the Medicare program. In addition, the political activity and mobilization of the near-old (50-64 years) is considered and compared with older and younger Americans. Finally, the changes in political behavior and mobilization attributed to defining older Americans as being 50 years of age or more are explored to determine whether the political behavior of the near-old more closely mirrors that of younger Americans or older Americans.

WHAT WE KNOW ABOUT THE POLITICAL ACTIVITY OF OLDER AMERICANS

Numerous studies have shown a positive correlation between age and voter turnout in presidential elections (Verba and Nie 1972; Wolfinger and Rosenstone 1980; Lammers 1983; Hudson and Strate 1985; Leighley and Nagler 1992).

Rosenstone and Hansen (1993) provide one of the most recent tests of the independent effect of age on participation in both electoral and governmental politics. Their pooled analysis of National Election Studies surveys from 1956 through 1988 supports the conclusion that political involvement deepens as individuals grow older. They note, "Except where participation taxes physical stamina, except where physical infirmity defeats experience, participation rises consistently with age" (141). Participation in activities such as voting, contributing money, and volunteering for a campaign or party rise until about age 75 and then declines. The only form of participation that drops after age 25 is trying to persuade others to vote for a particular candidate or party.[58] Rosenstone and

Hansen argue that the experience and other resources that come with living life explain why age is an independent, positive determinant of political participation. With experience comes knowledge about what to do and where to go to take part in elections.

In *The Political Behavior of the Elderly* (1994), Peterson and Somit use a variety of independent variables to analyze and predict the political behavior of Americans 60 years of age and older. While the broad range of variables they consider includes psychological, political, and social markers, they focus on the socio-economic variables suggested by Verba and Nie (1972). Peterson and Somit test their hypotheses using the 1987 General Social Survey.

Their results show that while life experiences (such as stress) have some effect on their index of political activity, basic demographic variables, such as income and education, are the dominant predictors of political participation for older adults.[59] Education, being male, and having group memberships, fewer siblings, political interest, and more life satisfaction explain their political participation index the most. These factors have direct, positive effects on and explain 46 percent of the variation in political activity.

In addition to the impact of the socio-economic variables, two variables of particular interest for health policy researchers capture the effect of health status. When Peterson and Somit combine education and health to indicate the "able elderly," the combination has a positive effect on the likelihood of political participation.[60] They also find that good health positively affects the likelihood of political participation among older women, a sizable portion of the older population. While Peterson and Somit's analysis did not confirm some of their own predicted relationships, their insights into the role of health as a predictor of political activity should inform models of political participation developed to explain the political behavior of older Americans.[61]

MODELING POLITICAL PARTICIPATION

Evidence suggests that models explaining participation for the population as a whole also explain participation for older Americans. The most comprehensive model explaining political participation, the civic voluntarism model (Verba, Schlozman, and Brady 1995), divides these determining factors into three primary categories subsequently described: resources, engagement, and

recruitment. The effect of each varies with the nature of the political activity of interest.

Participation in politics requires some combination of
resources, including money, time, skill, knowledge, and self-confi-
dence. People with more monetary and social resources are better
able to pay the costs of personal, political activity, and tend to participate more often.

More specifically, wealthy people vote, write letters, campaign,
and petition more than do poor people (Verba and Nie 1972;
Wolfinger and Rosenstone 1980; Rosenstone and Hansen 1993;
Verba, Schlozman, and Brady 1995). Poorer people must use their
money to pay for basic necessities such as rent, clothes, school sup-
plies for children, etc..

Another resource that activists invest in the political process is
time. The Verba, Schlozman, and Brady survey (1995) is unique in
its ability to capture this commodity. They ask respondents how
much free time they have and find that individuals who are not
working or who have a spouse who is not working tend to have
more time to invest in political activity. Thus, measures of employment and the employment of a spouse have an effect on the likelihood of participation when controlling for family income.

Education is another resource that facilitates political activity.
Educated people are more likely to participate in politics than less
educated people (Verba and Nie 1972; Wolfinger and Rosenstone
1980; Rosenstone and Hansen 1993; Verba, Schlozman, and
Brady 1995). In the U.S., educational experience may foster democratic values and nurture a sense of citizenship that encourages
participation. Education also enhances an individual's cognitive
skills, which enable them to collect and use the information needed
to register to vote or to develop a persuasive argument. Finally,
people with more education also are more likely to communicate
their political preferences effectively and have the confidence to do
so.

The final resources included in models of participation and discussed in this section are garnered from nonpolitical activities.
Civic skills developed from involvement with work, voluntary
associations, and religious institutions translate into skills needed
for political activities (Wolfinger and Rosenstone 1980; Verba,
Schlozman, and Brady 1995). Writing letters, chairing a meeting,
or persuading others to participate in events for these organiza-

tions enable activists to hone communication and organizational skills that can be used to write a letter to a Congressperson or persuade others to vote in a particular way.

The next major group of factors affecting political activity includes several measures of engagement in a political campaign. Political interest, political efficacy, political information, and partisanship are four often-used measures of engagement. For example, people with a sense of confidence in their own ability to understand and participate in politics (internal efficacy) as well as a sense that their political activities can influence what government does (external efficacy) tend to participate more in presidential elections (Rosenstone and Hansen 1993). Also, people who strongly support a political party, i.e. are partisan, are more likely to participate than people with weak preferences (Rosenstone and Hansen 1993; Verba, Schlozman, and Brady 1995).

The majority of resources, skills, and measures of issue engagement previously discussed represent characteristics of people that change slowly, if at all.[62] In contrast, as noted by Rosenstone and Hansen, "Both the level of political participation and the people who participate change significantly from month to month, year to year, election to election" (21). Along with the personal qualities and policy positions of candidates for office, opportunities offered by political parties and interest groups to attend forums or contribute money and time, etc. vary with the political environment. The final factors that influence a person's ability to be politically active, social and recruitment networks, help to explain fluctuations in activity across elections.

Most people belong to social networks of family, friends, neighbors, and co-workers who convey expectations about desirable and appropriate behaviors. Social networks reward members who act in the group's interest and convey information as their participants communicate and learn about politics from the group. Networks can create and enforce expectations that make effective, coordinated political action possible.[63]

Even with strong social networks that value political participation and effectively distribute political information, most people do not know enough about politics to participate in a manner congruent with their preferences. This information gap may be filled by political leaders (party officials, interest group leaders, and activists) who value citizen involvement as an important political resource, and thus, have an incentive to convey information and provide opportunities for political activity to citizens who can help win political battles. Rosenstone and Hansen (1993) call efforts to deploy citizen involvement "mobilization tactics," and describes these efforts as follows.

Mobilization occurs when the political actor has done something, directly or indirectly, to increase the likelihood of others' participation. Political leaders build organizations, such as political parties, that provide opportunities for people to contribute time and money to political causes. They also develop mechanisms to subsidize political information directly and in other ways offset the costs of participation for citizens.

Mobilization is costly, is not the only political resource, and is not always effective. Political leaders use this mechanism selectively by targeting particular people at particular times. As a rule, political leaders target their resources where they will motivate the most effective people in terms of candidate resources. For example, political actors are more likely to mobilize people they know than people they do not know. Acquaintances are easy to contact and are more likely to share the political interest of the actor than are strangers. Additionally, political leaders use social networks to mobilize citizens for political action to offset the cost of contacting individuals and to multiply the effects of direct mobilization.

Generally, politicians, political parties, advocates, and other activists are more likely to mobilize people who have power and who are likely to participate than people without these characteristics, specifically, people who are older, wealthier, educated, employed, belong to associations, and are easily identified as being part of a network. People with these characteristics are known by political leaders, their actions are more likely to produce favorable outcomes for political leaders, and they have more resources and receive more rewards from participation. As previously discussed, people who belong to well-defined, established social networks are more likely than other adults to be contacted. People who have lived in a community for a number of years, attend religious services, or own homes are more easily identified as part of a network and more easily contacted each year. Finally, for specific issues like Medicare, recipients of the policy at issue who have political resources, interests, and skills are also more likely than are other Americans to be contacted.

Along with deciding whom to mobilize, political actors must decide when to motivate citizens. In order for mobilization to effectively incite participation, citizens must have an interest in an issue or not be distracted by other concerns, and the issue must be part of the decision agenda (e.g., during an election or policy debate). Citizens are more likely to be mobilized or to participate in politics when salient issues are on the agenda (e.g., big pocketbook or moral issues). Salient issues affect people more directly and provide more incentive for people to respond to mobilization to protect an interest. For example, the prominence of ads concerning Medicare/Social Security in the 1996 presidential campaign suggests that political parties calculated that positions concerning Medicare would entice older adults to participate and vote in a particular way. Finally, people are more likely to be contacted when an important political decision, such as an impending vote during Medicare reform debates, is predicted to be decided by a close margin.

Opportunities for mobilization are key determinants of voter turnout and the likelihood that a person will attempt to persuade people in their social network to vote a particular way. One drawback of focusing on individual elections is that the small sample of participants in each election limits the number of activities that can be analyzed by age. The impact of age on the likelihood of being contacted by a political party is examined as a proxy for how age may affect other forms of participation such as volunteering for a campaign.

Based on the most recent theories of voter behavior, the following models are used to test hypotheses about the effect of age on turnout, persuasion, and mobilization.[64]

Voter Turnout/Persuasion=		Age
	Resources:	Education
		Employed
		Union membership
		Religious attendance
		Income
		Employed spouse
		+
	Engagement:	Care about outcome of election
		Attention to campaign on television
		Listen to campaign on radio
		Internal efficacy
		External efficacy
		Political knowledge
		Perceived political knowledge
		Partisanship
		+
	Recruitment:	Contact by political party
		+
	Social networks:	Years in community
		Homeowner
	+	
	Other variables:	Race
		Gender

Contact by Political Party =	Age
	Income
	Education
	Partisanship
	Years in community
	Religious attendance
	Homeowner
	Employed
	Race
	Gender
	Care about outcome of election

MEDICARE AS AN EMERGING ELECTION ISSUE

The 1996 presidential election provides a unique opportunity to examine voter turnout, attempts to persuade the vote of friends or family members, and mobilization efforts in the light of an election issue particularly salient for older Americans. The stage upon which Medicare emerged as an election issue in 1996 began to materialize several years earlier.

Until the 1990s, entitlement programs for older Americans were considered "the third rail" of politics. That is, one could consider changes to Medicare, but should not alter the program. Politicians, especially Democrats, believed that proposals designed to fundamentally change these programs would invoke the wrath of older Americans.[65] This perception was based, in part, on earlier political debates. For example in 1988 repeal of the Medicare Catastrophic Coverage Act (MCCA) within 18 months of its passage demonstrated how effectively older Americans and their advocates could lobby Congress and influence Medicare policy decisions.[66]

However, the political debate surrounding repeal of MCCA also highlighted the heterogeneity of needs and preferences among older Americans and the difficulty of representing their array of interests as a single block. The American Association of Retired Persons' (AARP) support for MCCA was countered with a campaign sponsored by other advocates for older Americans that galvanized the protests of Medicare recipients who would pay for catastrophic coverage and not receive additional benefits.[67] This unexpected and successful revolt weakened AARP's credibility as the representative of all older Americans, and its response to the subsequent debate about Medicare reflected its struggle to maintain credibility in an evolving political environment.

The primary change in the political environment that facilitated Medicare's prominent position on the electoral agenda in 1996 occurred in 1994. In the wake of the tide that swept Republicans into control of Congress, Republicans heralded balancing the federal budget as a top item on the political agenda of the Congress and the President of the United States. This political reality and an April 1995 report of the Medicare Trustees that projected the insolvency of the Hospital Insurance Trust Fund by the year 2002

if no preventive actions were taken inspired Republicans to propose significant changes to the Medicare program.[68]

The 1995 debates about how to change Medicare's level of
spending pitted Speaker Newt Gingrich and a large class of conservative, freshman Congressional Republicans against President
Clinton and Congressional Democrats.[69] Despite containing the
largest proposed changes to the Medicare program since its incep-
tion in 1965, the primary opposition to the Republican plan came
from Democrats and not interest groups. Speaker Gingrich worked
closely with health care groups and crafted a plan that would
appease doctors, hospitals, and health insurers. For example, limited payments to doctors and hospitals were accompanied by support for allowing provider-sponsored networks to contract with
Medicare.

Using the game plan that avoided direct opposition from the
health care industry, Speaker Gingrich was able to deflect the initial criticism of the AARP by combining an expansion in the range
of health plan options and benefits with increased costs for some
choices. The plan included various incentives to encourage
Medicare beneficiaries to join lower cost health plans, such as
health maintenance organizations, or to establish medical savings
accounts that would help protect against major medical costs.
Additionally, private, non-Medicare, fee-for-service plans or
HMOs in which the Medicare beneficiary used services outside of
the designated network could bill recipients for the full balance of
the bill, a practice previously capped. Finally, monthly premiums
paid for physician services (Medicare Part B) would stay at the current level and the wealthiest beneficiaries would pay the entire cost
of Medicare Part B coverage. The total package of proposed costs
and benefits would have affected the choices of every Medicare
beneficiary.

The lack of a major interest group campaign against the
Republican proposal did not negate significant concerns that
would become the basis for campaign ads in the 1996 election. The
Congressional Quarterly Almanac reported that, "[Some] health
care experts said the reductions would substantially affect the
access, eligibility and out-of-pocket expenses of Medicare beneficiaries, and they were expected to result in more people moving into
lower-cost managed-care plans that restricted access to doctors
and technology" (7-3). Critics of the medical savings accounts

(MSAs) predicted that costs for HMOs, traditional fee-for-service providers, and eventually premiums would rise as healthy seniors who currently balance the costs of sicker people disproportionately selected the MSAs.[70]

The Republican-led restructuring of Medicare passed both houses of Congress as part of a massive budget reconciliation bill that President Clinton vetoed on December 6, 1995.

MEDICARE IN THE 1996 PRESIDENTIAL ELECTION

The 1995 budget drama, in which Medicare played a starring role, provided partisan rhetorical fodder for the 1996 presidential campaigns. Republicans vowed to "preserve, protect, and strengthen" Medicare for future generations (Weisskopf and Maraniss 1995). Democrats charged Republicans with 'balancing the budget on the backs of the elderly' (Congressional Quarterly 1995).

In the presidential campaign, divisions between the political parties highlighted by the budget process were used primarily in a preemptive strike by the Clinton campaign before Senator Robert Dole was chosen as the Republican presidential nominee in the spring of 1996 (West 1997). Beginning as early as mid-March 1995, the Democratic National Committee spent $15 million in ads promoting President Clinton's 1996 reelection bid by capitalizing on Republicans' attempts to change Medicare and the federal budget. President Clinton was portrayed as the remaining safeguard against a Republican revolution that would eviscerate federal programs such as Medicare and Medicaid and the primary proponent of efforts to bolster education and the environment. Once the campaign pitted President Clinton against Bob Dole, the Clinton campaign switched to other issues.

Portions of the electorate also were bombarded with reminders of the Medicare debate aimed at Congressional candidates (Corrado 1996). The AFL-CIO spent close to $35 million for advertising and extensive organizing activities targeted primarily at decreasing support for freshman Republicans. The ads primarily conveyed negative portrayals of Republicans' positions on health care, education, and the minimum wage. The Republican National Committee (RNC) and the National Republican Congressional Committee (NRCC) responded to labor's blitz with campaigns of their own. For example, in August of 1996 the NRCC ran a series of ads designed to fend off attacks on their efforts to restructure

Medicare. According to Corrado (1996), this $8 million issue advocacy campaign was designed to aid potentially vulnerable incumbents in thirty congressional districts.

That the 1995-96 ad campaigns utilized rhetoric from the 1995 federal budget debates suggests that Democrats and their allies wanted the Republicans' proposed changes to government programs, especially Medicare, to become voting issues for the electorate. One measure of issues that likely affect vote choice is taken via surveys of people as they exit the voting area. Exit polls taken in 1996 show voters indicated that Medicare/Social Security was one of the top voting issues, a place these issues had not occupied in the previous two elections (Blendon, et al. 1992, 1997). In 1988, the top three issues in the presidential election as measured by exit polls were the economy/jobs, national defense, and taxes. In 1992, the economy/jobs were followed by the deficit and health care. In 1996, Medicare/Social Security and education followed the top issue from the past two presidential elections.

Finally, public opinion polling conducted soon after the 1996 election suggested that while Medicare/Social Security was the second highest ranked voting issue for all Americans in 1996, these programs had particular salience for older Americans. For example, Blendon, et al. (1997) report that Medicare/Social Security was the top-ranked issue among voters aged 60 years of age and older. Almost one-third (29%) of older Americans ranked this combination as the top issue while only eight percent of voters younger than 30 years of age cited the issue.

Recognizing the difficulty of discerning factors that determine a vote, the evidence in this section supports the argument that Medicare was a top voting issue in 1996, especially for older Americans. The following hypotheses reflect this information.

HYPOTHESES

In contrast to the dominance of the economy on the campaign agenda of 1992, the political campaigns of both 1988 and 1996 centered on a broader range of issues (Corrado 1996). The 1996 campaign was unique among these elections in that the 1995 Republican plan to restructure Medicare became a critical element of President Clinton's early efforts to frame the election as a referendum on the 1994 "Republican Revolution." President Clinton continually reminded voters of Republicans' uncaring and insensitive attempts to "cut Medicare," "slash education," and "gut the environment" (West 1997). According to the pre-election and exit polls previously discussed, Americans, especially older Americans, took notice. The following hypotheses reflect patterns in political behavior that may have resulted from Medicare's role in the 1996 election:

Hypothesis 1: *Ceteris paribus*, in 1996, the difference between the likelihood of voting for Americans 65 years of age or older and the likelihood for younger Americans was larger than the difference in 1988 or 1992.

Hypothesis 2: *Ceteris paribus*, in 1996, the difference in the likelihood of attempting to persuade others to vote for a particular candidate or political party for Americans 65 years of age or older and the likelihood for younger Americans was larger than the difference in 1988 or 1992.

Hypothesis 3: *Ceteris paribus*, the difference between the likelihood of being contacted by a political party for Americans 65 years of age or older and the likelihood for younger Americans was larger than the difference in 1988 or 1992.

The following section begins the test of these hypotheses with discussion of the data and methods used in this study.

DATA AND METHODS[71]

The data for this analysis are components of a series of surveys known as the American National Election Studies (ANES) conducted by the Center for Political Studies at the University of Michigan. The study population is defined as all U.S. citizens of voting age on or before the respective election day and residing in housing units in the 48 coterminous states.[72] Until 1992, all respondents for each survey were interviewed in person. Subsequent surveys employed a mix of in-person and telephone modes.[73] The ANES are based on a multi-stage area probability sample described in the codebook for each year.

Several ANES surveys include a combination of respondents who participated in previous surveys and an additional sample from the current year. Also, some of the questions are asked before each election and others administered after each election. Because the model includes variables collected before and after each election, this analysis includes respondents who were interviewed on both occasions.

For each year of the study, the final sample included people interviewed both before and after the presidential election of that year. In the 1988 ANES (Miller and the National Election Studies 1989), 2,040 interviews were completed before the election with a response rate of 70.5 percent. The post-election interviews were conducted with 1,775 respondents and a response rate of 87 percent. The 1988 sample for this analysis contains 1,772 respondents.[74] In 1992 (Miller, et al. 1993) and 1996 (Rosenstone, et al. 1997) panels drawn from previous periods were interviewed again along with additional samples. In 1992, 2,487 adults were interviewed before the election with a response rate ranging from 69.2 percent to 77.7 percent.[75] After the election, 2,255 people were interviewed with a response rate ranging from 85 - 91.8 percent.[76] The 1992 sample size for this analysis is 2,255. In 1996, three-fourths of the respondents were first interviewed in 1992 or 1994. In total, 1,714 peolple were interviewed before the election with a response rate of 71 percent. The 1,534 post-election interviews had a response rate of 90 percent. The 1996 sample for this analysis contains 1,534 respondents.

The ANES surveys have a complex sampling design created to ensure that every household has an equal probability of selection.[77] The resulting samples, in recent elections, are then weighted to adjust for the unequal probability of selection for adults due to the varying number of adults eligible for the survey in each household. Based on the sample size of each survey included in this study, one can say with a 95 percent level of confidence that the error due to random sampling is +/- two percent. Other sources of error that may affect the validity of the results include nonresponse bias (which is addressed with weights in 1992 and 1996) and question wording and ordering effects, all of which are difficult to measure.

Three methods are used to analyze these data and test the hypotheses. First, bivariate percentage distributions of political activity and mobilization within age categories are compared for the last three presidential elections. [78,79]

Second, Verba, Schlozman, and Brady's (1995) Logged Representation Scale (LRS) is used to show how well the mix of age groups among activists and recruits mirrors the distribution of the groups among the general population. The LRS is the log of the ratio of the percentage of activists who have a particular characteristic divided by the percentage of adults in the general public who have the same characteristic. For example, 60 percent of voters in 1988 were 49 years of age or younger and 64 percent of adults belong in this category. The LRS for this example is ln(60/64) = -0.06. The LRS indicates the extent to which the age groups are over- or underrepresented in the population as indicated by a positive or negative score, respectively. A score of zero indicates representation equal to that in the general population. As a guide to the actual amount of the representation, a score of 0.30 indicates that activists are twice as likely as a member of the general population to belong to a particular age group.

Finally, logistic regressions test whether the impact of age on the likelihood of participation and mobilization in 1996 differs significantly from its impact in 1988 or 1992. Odds ratios are used to compare effects across presidential elections, and confidence intervals are used to test for significant differences between the ratios. The odds ratio shows the likelihood of voting for an older age group when compared with adults 64 years old or younger, controlling for other factors. A ratio of one indicates that both groups have the same likelihood of voting.

While descriptive statistics showing the rates of participation and mobilization during the past 10 presidential elections provide context for this analysis, the primary focus of this study is on the age groups that existed within the unique context of each of the past three elections. This type of cross-sectional analysis has disadvantages for explaining the effects of aging on voter turnout, political persuasion, and mobilization.

For example, several explanations, often interlinked, exist to explain differences in political behavior between different age groups: 1) Life-cycle effect- At each stage in the aging process, from childhood to older adulthood, individuals have different needs and interests that reflect changes in physiology, cognitive functioning, and emotional patterns and may result in different policy preferences (Braungart and Braungart 1986); 2) Generational or cohort effect- Significant cultural and historical influences bind members of a generation together and separate them from younger and older generations (Braungart and Braungart 1986). Thus, "baby boomers" may react differently to social policy or identify themselves as a member of this group not because of their biological age, but because they, for example, experienced Vietnam at a particular stage in their development unique from younger or older cohorts. Also, generational differences may be caused by the socialization of parents, grandparents or offspring; and, 3) Unique stake- Rational choice models that explain political behavior in terms of costs and benefits suggest that the immediate benefit that older Americans have or will have from Medicare would be a unique incentive for them to act that would not factor into the decision-making process of younger Americans. While this study is motivated by this third explanation, cross-sectional research designs are not able to reveal which combination of these factors explains the results.

RESULTS

In the past three presidential elections, the percentage of people who reported voting has not changed by a large amount. In 1988, 70 percent of adults surveyed claimed to have voted compared to 76 percent in 1992 and 72 percent in 1996 (Figure 12). The six percentage point increase in turnout from 1988 to 1992 and the four percentage point decline between 1992 and 1996 are significant but slight and mirror the actual voter turnout reported by the Election Research Center in the *Statistical Abstract of the United States* (U.S. Bureau of the Census 1996).[80]

The percentage of all Americans who attempted to persuade someone in a presidential election increased nine percentage points from 30 percent in 1988 to 39 percent in 1992, the highest rate in presidential elections since 1960 (Figure 13).[81] In 1996, the percentage of adults who attempted to persuade someone because of the election was 27.

The most recent presidential election prompted political parties to increase their efforts to contact Americans, especially compared with their activity in 1992. In 1992, a political party contacted 21

percent of Americans. In 1996, a small but significant increase
raised this figure to 27 percent (Figure 14).

Figure 12: Voter Turnout in Presidential Elections

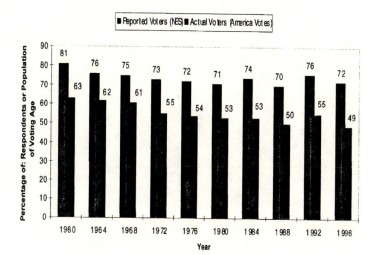

Figure13: Percentage of Americans Attempting to Persuade in
Presidential Elections

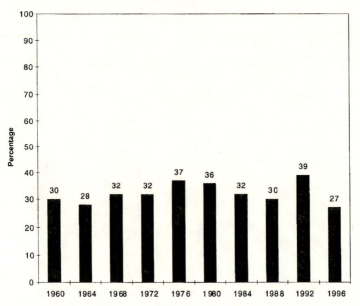

Figur 14: Percentage of Americans Contacted by Political Party in
Presidential Elections

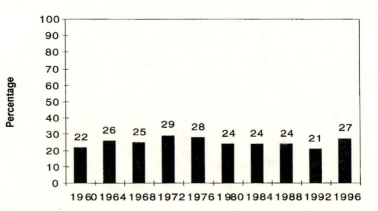

This study focuses on the change in distribution of political activity and mobilization across three presidential election years. Table 14 shows the distribution of participation and mobilization among the age categories for each election year. For each year, I calculated the difference in the percentage of voters in each age group. For example, in 1988, 66 percent of adults 49 years old or younger and 78 percent of adults 65 years old or older voted in the presidential election. The difference in these percentages is 12 percentage points.[82] By comparison, this difference was 11 in 1992 and 17 in 1996. Similarly, the difference in distributions for attempting to persuade someone were -10 in 1988, -16 in 1992, and zero in 1996. Both sets of trends suggest that older Americans may have had an even greater relative likelihood of participating in 1996 than in the previous two presidential elections.

The comparisons of differences for percentage of people recruited during presidential elections vary in comparison with the previously discussed comparisons. The differences for being mobilized were 15, six, and 16 in 1988, 1992, and 1996, respectively. This suggests that the relative distributions of mobilization were similar in 1996 and 1992.

When comparing the distributions of political activity and mobilization for the near-old and the youngest group of adults, the trends are similar to the previous comparisons with interesting differences. For example, the differences for being contacted by a political party were seven in 1988, eight in 1992, and nine in 1996.

Table 14: Percentage Distribution of Political Activity and Mobilization within Age Groups

Dependent Variable	Age <= 49 years			Age 50-64			Age > = 65 years		
	1988	1992	1996	1988	1992	1996	1988	1992	1996
Vote									
Yes	66%	73%	66%	79%	84%	80%	78%	84%	83%
No	34	27	34	21	16	20	22	16	17
Persuade									
Yes	32%	42%	26%	28%	37%	35%	22%	26%	26%
No	68	58	74	72	63	65	78	74	74
Mobilized									
Yes	20%	18%	23%	27%	26%	32%	35%	24%	39%
No	80	82	77	73	73	61	65	76	61

Another perspective from which to consider rates of participation and mobilization is to determine the level of representation among the different age groups. Comparing the representation among voters of the youngest age group, the middle group, and the oldest group reveals that the middle group was not more over-represented in 1996 compared to the previous two years (Figure 15). The middle group was over-represented to a similar degree in each year. The oldest group, however, was more over-represented among voters in 1996. The LRS score for this group in 1988 was 0.06 which increased to 0.12 in 1992 and to 0.16 in 1996 (the highest score for the oldest Americans in the past 10 elections).

The more dramatic shifts in representation occurred among persuaders (Figure 16). The middle age group shifted from being under-represented in 1988 (score of -0.05) and 1992 (score of -0.06), to being over-represented with a score of 0.23 in 1996 (the highest score for this group in a presidential election since 1960). The LRS score in 1996 for the oldest adults suggests the least level of under-representation for this group in the past 10 presidential elections. The -0.37 score for the oldest Americans in 1988 and 1992 shifted to -0.06 in 1996.

Finally, efforts to mobilize the various age groups resulted in 1992 having the largest amount of over-representation among the middle age group, with the score for 1996 the second largest (Figure 17). Efforts to mobilize the oldest Americans were reflected in the largest score for this group (0.39) in 1996 than in any other presidential year since 1960.

Americans 65 years of age and older were more over-represented among voters, persuaders, and people contacted by a political party in 1996 than in 1988 or 1992.

With this measure, the results for the near-old differed from those of the oldest group of Americans. People in the near-old category were not more over-represented among voters in 1996 than in 1988 or 1992, and they were dramatically over-represented among persuaders in 1996 compared with their under-representation in 1988 and 1992.

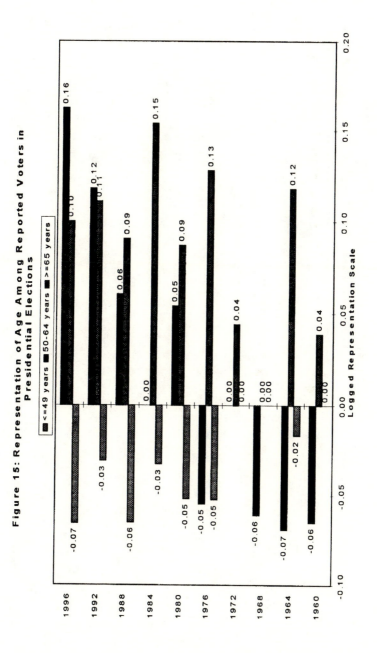

Figure 15: Representation of Age Among Reported Voters in Presidential Elections

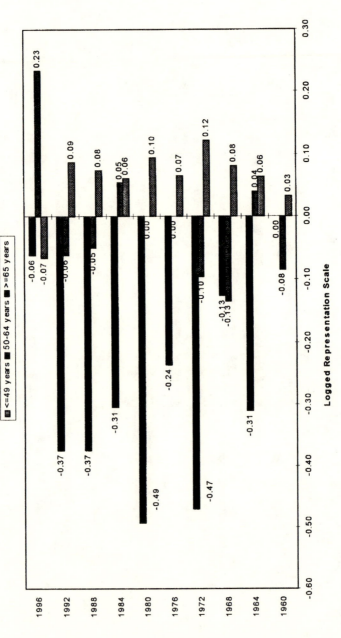

Figure 16: Representation of Age Among Persuaders in Presidential Elections

Figure 17: Representation of Age Among Recruited in Presidential Elections

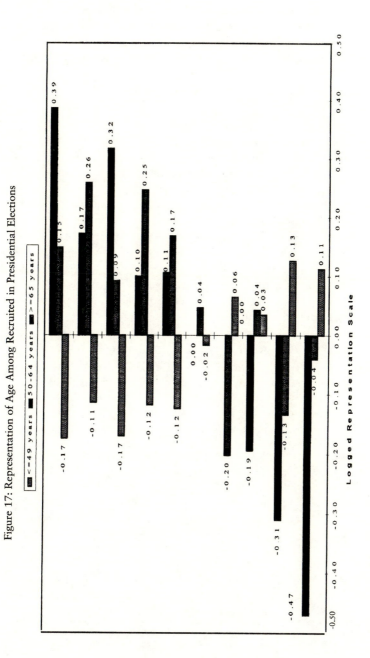

The descriptive statistics suggest that a politician with a bird's eye view of political activists and people whom the political parties deemed likely candidates for political activity generally would have seen a different picture in 1996 than in 1988 or 1992. Next, the impact of age on political activity and mobilization is examined when controlling for other determinants of these political acts.

The effects of age on the likelihood of voting, persuading, or being contacted by a political party will be discussed in terms of the odds ratio for the effect. Hypothesis one anticipates that the odds ratios for 1996 were significantly larger than the ratios in 1992 or 1988.

There was a significant effect of age on the likelihood of voting in the last three presidential elections (Table 15).[83] In each election, members of the oldest group of Americans (65 years of age and older) were at least one and one-half times more likely than were Americans 64 years of age or younger to vote.

A comparison of the odds ratios for each presidential election shows mixed support for the first hypothesis. The 95 percent confidence interval surrounding the odds ratio for 1996 includes the odds ratio for 1992 and does not include the ratio for 1988. In 1996, older Americans were 2.26 times more likely to vote than younger Americans. In 1988, this ratio was one. The comparison between 1996 and 1992 shows no significant difference in the ratios.

Table 15: Logit Parameter Estimates for the Likelihood of Reporting a Vote in Presidential Elections (Total Population)

	1988 Estimated Coeff. SE	Odds Ratio	1992 Estimated Coeff. SE	Odds Ratio	1996 Estimated Coeff. SE	Odds Ratio
	(n=1435)		(n=1876)		(n=1372)	
constant	-1.73* 0.48	---	-1.26* 0.31	---	-0.83* 0.37	---
Age <=64 (ref)						
Age 65+	0.46 0.28	1.59	0.60* 0.22	1.82*	0.82* 0.31	2.26*

Notes: 1) model = age + education, employed, union, religion, income, employed spouse, years in community, homeownership, race, gender, care about outcome of election, attention to campaign on television, listen to campaign on radio, perceived knowledge, partisanship, internal efficacy, external efficacy, political knowledge, and contacted by political party, 2) * p < = 0.05.

As expected from previous analyses, older Americans were less likely to attempt to persuade someone than other Americans in 1988 and 1992 (Table 16). For example, in 1988 older Americans were 0.62 as likely than those under 65 to attempt to persuade others. The ratio in 1996 supports the second hypothesis. The older group was even more likely to attempt persuasion other in 1996 than in 1988 or 1992. In 1996, there was no significant difference in the likelihood of persuading for older and younger Americans, so the odds ratio was one. In 1988, older Americans were 0.62 as likely than younger Americans to attempt to persuade someone to vote a particular way, and in 1992, the ratio was 0.37.

Table 16: LogitParameter Estimates for the Likelihood of Attempting to Persuade Others to Vote a Particular Way in Presidential Elections (Total Population)

	1988 Estimated Coeff. SE	Odds Ratio	1992 Estimated Coeff SE	Odds Ratio	1996 Estimated Coeff SE	Odds Ratio
	(n=1436)		(n=1876)		(n=1372)	
constant	-1.99* 0.41	---	0.76* 0.31	---	-1.97* 0.43	---
Age <=64 (ref)						
Age 65+	-0.48 0.20	0.62*	-0.98* 0.20	0.37*	-0.29* 0.25	0.75

Notes: 1) model = age + education, employed, union, religion, income, employed spouse, years in community, homeownership, race, gender, care about outcome of election, attention to campaign on television, listen to campaign on radio, perceived knowledge, partisanship, internal efficacy, external efficacy, political knowledge, and contacted by political party, 2) * p <= 0.05.

The ratios for the effect of age on mobilization efforts present mixed confirmation of the third hypothesis (Table 17). In 1996,

Table 17: Logit Parameter for the Likelihood of Being Contacted by a Political Party in Presidential Elections (Total Population)

	1988 Estimated Coeff. SE	Odds Ratio	1992 Estimated Coeff SE	Odds Ratio	1996 Estimated Coeff SE	Odds Ratio
	(n=1422)		(n=1887)		(n=1378)	
constant	-2.44* 0.36	---	-2.17 0.28	---	-2.58* 0.40	---
Age <=64 (ref)						
Age 65+	0.73* 0.23	2.07*	0.21 0.20	1.24	0.64* 0.21	1.90*

Notes: 1) model = age + income, education, partnership, years in community, religeon, homeownership, employed, race, gender, care about outcome of election, 2) * p <= 0.05.

the ratio was significantly larger than the ratio in 1992 but no different in a similar comparison with 1988. Older Americans were 1.90 times more likely to be contacted in 1996. In 1992, there was no significant difference in the likelihood of being contacted by a political party for the two age groups.

The next issue for analysis is whether or not the previous comparisons were distributed evenly among segments of the population.[84] Generally, campaign ads are targeted to energize core constituents and to persuade undecided and independent voters to favor a particular candidate. Thus, in 1996 older Americans who were also Democrats and Independents should have been especially motivated and inspired to participate in 1996, in part, because of previously discussed ad campaigns sponsored by the Democratic Party and supporters. For more insight into previously discussed relationships, the following tables include regressions among people who identified themselves as Democrats and Independents (Tables 18-23).

Contrary to the general population in which older Americans were more likely to vote, among Democrats there was no difference in the likelihood of voting for the two age groups in any election year studied (Table 18). In contrast to Democrats and in

Table 18: Logit Parameter Estimates for the Likelihood of Reporting a Vote in Presidential Elections (Democrats Only)

	1988 Estimated Coeff. SE	Odds Ratio	1992 Estimated Coeff. SE	Odds Ratio	1996 Estimated Coeff. SE	Odds Ratio
	(n=518)		(n=660)		(n=543)	
constant	-1.79* 0.74	---	-1.48 0.54	---	-0.98 0.74	---
Age <=64 (ref)						
Age 65+	-0.10 0.44	0.91	0.66 0.39	1.94	0.77 0.48	2.17

Notes: 1) model = age + education, employed, union, religion, income, employed spouse, years in community, homeownership, race, gender, care about outcome of election, attention to campaign on television, listen to campaign on radio, perceived knowledge, partisanship, internal efficacy, external efficacy, political knowledge, and contacted by political party, 2) * p < = 0.05.

comparison with the general population, among Independents in 1988 and 1992, older Americans were close to two and one half times more likely (ratios of 2.25 and 2.46, respectively) than younger Americans to vote (Table 19). Among Independents in 1996, older Americans were more than four times more likely than younger adults to vote. For both of these political groups the odds ratios in 1988 and 1992 are not significantly different from the ratio in 1996.

Table 19: Logit Parameter Estimates for the Likelihood of Reporting a Vote in Presidential Elections (Independents Only)

	1988 Estimated Coeff. SE	Odds Ratio	1992 Estimated Coeff SE	Odds Ratio	1996 Estimated Coeff SE	Odds Ratio
	(n=434)		(n=631)		(n=353)	
constant	-3.00* 0.60	—	-2.28* 0.53	—	-1.78* 0.66	—
Age <=64 (ref)						
Age 65+	-0.81* 0.42	2.25*	0.90* 0.36	2.46*	1.48* 0.63	4.39*

Notes: 1) model = age + education, employed, union, religion, income, employed spouse, years in community, homeownership, race, gender, care about outcome of election, attention to campaign on television, listen to campaign on radio, perceived knowledge, partisanship, internal efficacy, external efficacy, political knowledge, and contacted by political party, 2) * p <= 0.05.

In the general population, older Americans were less likely than younger Americans to attempt to persuade in 1988 and 1992. Among Democrats the trends for the full population are not repeated (Table 20). During every election, there was no difference in the likelihood of persuading for older and younger Americans. Among Independents, older Americans were less likely to persuade in 1992, and there was no difference in their likelihood of persuading in 1988 or 1992 (Table 21).

Table 20: Logit Parameter Estimates for the Likelihood of Attempting to Persuade
Others to Vote a Particular Way in Presidential Elections (Democrats Only)

	1988 Estimated Coeff. SE	Odds Ratio	1992 Estimated Coeff SE	Odds Ratio	1996 Estimated Coeff SE	Odds Ratio
	(n=517)		(n=660)		(n=543)	
constant	-3.18* 0.73	—	-1.65* 0.59	—	-1.49* 0.75	—
Age <=64 (ref)						
Age 65+	-0.01 0.33	0.99	-0.59 0.32	0.55	-0.35 0.51	0.71

Notes: 1) model = age + education, employed, union, religion, income, employed spouse, years in community,
homeownership, race, gender, care about outcome of election, attention to campaign on television, listen to
campaign on radio, perceived knowledge, partisanship, internal efficacy, external efficacy, political knowledge,
and contacted by political party, 2) * p <= 0.05.

Table 21: Logit Parameter Estimates for the Likelihood of Attempting to Persuade Others to
Vote a Particular Way in Presidential Elections (Independents Only)

	1988 Estimated Coeff. SE	Odds Ratio	1992 Estimated Coeff. SE	Odds Ratio	1996 Estimated Coeff. SE	Odds Ratio
	(n=435)		(n=631)		(n=353)	
constant	-3.28* 0.93	---	-1.07* 0.42	---	-2.67* 0.82	---
Age <=64 (ref)						
Age 65+	-0.36 0.52	0.70	-1.11* 0.40	0.33*	-0.42* 0.50	0.66

Notes: 1) model = age + education, employed, union, religion, income, employed spouse, years in community,
homeownership, race, gender, care about outcome of election, attention to campaign on television, listen to
campaign on radio, perceived knowledge, partisanship, internal efficacy, external efficacy, political knowledge,
and contacted by political party, 2) * p < = 0.05.

Independents did show mixed support for the second hypothesis. In 1996, the odds ratio comparing the likelihood of persuading for older and younger Americans was one. In 1992, older
Americans were less likely than younger Americans to attempt to
persuade someone.

In the general population, 1996 did spur a larger differential
rate of mobilization for the two age groups when compared with
the rates in 1992. This support of the third hypothesis also
occurred among Democrats (Table 22). In 1992, there was no difference in the likelihood of being contacted for older Americans

Table 22: Logit Parameter Estimates for the Likelihood of Being Contacted by a Political Party in Presidential Elections (Democrats Only)

	1988		1992		1996	
	Estimated Coeff. SE	Odds Ratio	Estimated Coeff. SE	Odds Ratio	Estimated Coeff. SE	Odds Ratio
	(n=519)		(n=663)		(n=548)	
constant	-3.40* 0.58	---	-2.09* 0.44	---	-3.00* 0.68	---
Age <=64 (ref)						
Age 65+	0.85* 0.30	2.34*	0.18* 0.28	1.20	1.14* 0.36	3.12*

Notes: 1) model = age + income, education, partisanship, years in community, religeon, homeownership, employed, race, gender, care about outcome of election, 2) * p < = 0.05.

and younger Americans who identified themselves as Democrats. In 1996, older Americans in the Democratic party were three times more likely to be contacted.

For Independents, the only significant difference in the likelihood of being contacted occurred in 1996 (Table 23). In 1996, older Americans were 2.74 times more likely than younger Americans to be contacted by a political party. The ratio for 1996 was statistically different from the ratios in 1988 and 1992, which were zero.

Table 23: Logit Parameter Estimates for the Likelihood of Being Contacted by a Political Party in Presidential Elections (Independents Only)

	1988		1992		1996	
	Estimated Coeff. SE	Odds Ratio	Estimated Coeff. SE	Odds Ratio	Estimated Coeff. SE	Odds Ratio
	(n=435)		(n=636)		(n=354)	
constant	-2.14* 0.64	---	-2.64* 0.44	---	-2.46* 0.69	---
Age <=64 (ref)						
Age 65+	0.56 0.40	1.76	0.43* 0.37	1.53*	1.01* 0.44	2.74*

Notes: 1) model = age + income, education, partisanship, years in community, religeon, homeownership, race, gender, care about outcome of election, 2) * p < = 0.05.

THE IMPACT OF REDEFINING "OLDER AMERICANS"

All of the analyses previously discussed were also performed on models in which older Americans were defined as being at least 50 years of age, and in which dummy variables for 65 years of age and more and 50-64 years of age were included. The results of these analyses, available upon request, demonstrate that, generally, Americans in the near-old category tend to behave more like (not exactly like) older Americans than younger Americans. Where older Americans were more likely to participate or be contacted than Americans 49 years of age and younger, near-old Americans were also. Where there was no statistical difference between the people 65 years of age and older and adults 49 years of age and younger, there was no difference between the near-old and adults 49 years of age and younger. Accordingly, defining older Americans more broadly did not significantly change the results as they apply to the hypotheses tested here.

DISCUSSION/IMPLICATIONS

The purpose of this study was to determine how the rate of political activity of older Americans in 1996 differed from similar activities in 1988 and 1992. A secondary goal was to explore how sensitive the results are to a broader definition of older Americans.

The descriptive results suggest that politicians who pay attention to the political activity of older Americans did see a different distribution of activity in 1996, especially compared with their proportion in the population. Additionally, political parties seemingly targeted older Americans because of their age even more in 1996 than they did in 1988 or 1992. Thus, the popular perception of the influence of older Americans on the political system is likely to remain, and perhaps be strengthened in future elections.

Multivariate analyses controlling for other explanations of political activity suggests that the independent impact of age in 1996 was significantly different from its effect in two of the three comparisons in 1988 and 1992. Compared with the political activity of older Americans in 1988, adults 65 years of age and older were even more politically active in 1996. In contrast, the rate of mobilization in 1988 and 1996 did not differ. When compared with 1992, older Americans in 1996 were even more likely to persuade and to be mobilized, but not more likely to vote. In summary, the political environment in 1996 did seem to stimulate different rates of political participation among older Americans. The results were mixed for the efforts of political parties.

With regard to defining old age, Americans close in age to Medicare beneficiaries tended to behave in a manner similar to older Americans across the most recent presidential elections. Additional research could establish the sensitivity of these results to specific chronological demarcations between older and younger Americans.

By the year 2010, the elderly population is predicted to be twice as large as its current size and a larger percentage of the total population (Moon 1997). Because recent presidential elections have not disavowed politicians and media of the perception that older Americans exert influence on the political system as a group, politicians are likely to respond to a surge in the size of this politically active group by addressing issues particularly salient to them. Thus, issues such as Medicare, home health aide, or assistive technology will likely be increasingly prominent issues on campaign agendas in the next decade. These results suggest that any influence that older Americans exert on political outcomes via political participation inspired by these issues will also increase in the next decade.

Notes

[56]   Binstock (1992) and Rhodebeck (1993) discuss conditions that support political cohesion among older people and conditions that undermine this cohesion. For example, the population of older Americans contains a heterogeneous mix of income, education, employment experience, etc. that, along with age, also determine individual preferences. Alternatively, retirement communities may foster a sense of communal identity and common political interests.

[57]   Verba, Schlozman, and Brady likely would not include persuasion as a mode of political activity because the act is not directed toward an elected official. I include persuasion because numerous political scientists, including Rosenstone and Hansen (1993), have studied changes in this activity as part of a broader definition of political participation.

[58]   Rosenstone and Hansen offer the explanation that younger people have less experience with other people's biases and beliefs and more faith that they can change them.

[59]   Political activities included campaign work, communal politics, and voter turnout.

[60]   The designation of an able-elderly may be significant in determining the impact of older Americans on electoral politics depending on the future health of the "baby boom" cohort. One prediction is that a larger, healthier older cohort will become increasingly politically active and have a greater voice in public affairs than the current older cohorts (Peterson and Somit 1994). The alternative argument suggests that fewer sickly people will die earlier and the numbers of sick older people will accumulate (Peterson and Somit 1994). The resulting increase in the proportion of sick, older Americans and in the proportion of old-age morbidity will decrease the rate of political participation among all older Americans. Trend analyses incorporating measures of health would help to reveal either phenomenon.

[61]   This may be due to small samples for some of the questions. They only used one year and some of the subgroups are quite small. For this sample and model, age did not have an independent effect on political participation.

[62]   This section drawn from Chapter 2 of Rosenstone and Hansen (1993).

[63]   A significant contribution to our understanding of political participation would be to expand our understanding of the social networks of older adults. Do the networks of older people differ from those of younger

people? If so how? As the proportion of older Americans grows and their options for living arrangements change and expand, will these networks change? If so how? What are the implications for political mobilization and participation?

[64] Like age, race and sex are politically relevant characteristics of the population that can predict different political attitudes and behavior. Additionally, each variable (except for years in the community) is divided into dummy variables for the analyses. The coding and reference categories are defined in Tables B1-B3 in the Appendix. The distribution of the sample among the categories is described in Tables B4-B6 in the Appendix.

[65] Peterson and Somit (1993) note, "This perception is so strong that when administration spokespersons hinted at a possible freeze in federal Social Security COLA (cost of living allowance) payments in early 1993, Senator Daniel Patrick Moynihan spoke scathingly of President Clinton's 'death wish'" (7).

[66] The Medicare Catastrophic Coverage Act was designed to help older and disabled Americans pay for the high costs of medical care not covered by Medicare. Conflict ensued over the fact that the overwhelming majority of Medicare recipients would have had to pay an income surtax that would have funded additional coverage for a small minority of Medicare recipients who could not afford supplemental policies and did not qualify for Medicaid (Himelfarb 1995).

[67] AARP is the largest organization representing Americans 50 years of age and older.

[68] With $178 billion in costs, Medicare was 11 percent of the total federal budget in 1995. Medicare was 21.2 percent of mandatory spending in the federal budget in 1995 (The Henry J. Kaiser Family Foundation 1995).

[69] The remaining portions of this section are based on a synopsis of the Medicare debate in 1995 published in the *Congressional Quarterly Almanac* (1995).

[70] Concern for the size of the proposed changes in spending and the timetable for implementation prompted AARP to run ads against later versions of the plan.

[71] Information describing the data is based on the codebook for each election year.

[72] Housing units do not include military reservations.

[73] Up to 11 percent of the respondents in 1992 were interviewed by phone. In 1996, 47 respondents were interviewed by phone in the pre-election survey because they moved out of range of the interviewers. In the

1996 post-election survey, one-half of the respondents were randomly assigned to be interviewed by telephone.

[74] Per instructions in the codebook, three observations were dropped.

[75] The response rates depend on whether the respondent was part of the panel or cross-section and whether the interview was pre- or post-election.

[76] In addition to the previous note, in 1992, a response rate also considered whether a short-form was used for respondents who had moved to areas where SRC interviewers were no longer on staff. Forty-three respondents fell into this category.

[77] To control for design effects that could inflate standard error calculations, the survey commands in STATA were used to identify strata and primary sampling units (PSU). The census regions were identified as the strata and the primary sampling units identified by NES were designated the PSU.

[78] Two different types of statistical weights are incorporated into this analysis. Since 1956 the NES has impaneled groups for several years and added cross-sectional samples to replace panel members and to enhance the sample. After the initial survey of a panel, subsequent data collected from a panel is corrected for panel attrition and for the aging of panel respondents. For this analysis, descriptive statistics that compare variables from 1960-1996 elections are weighted in the later years of a panel (1960, 1976, 1992, and 1996) and unweighted otherwise. The cross-sectional analyses, both descriptive and multivariate, use weights provided by NES to adjust for several factors. The 1988 data are weighted by the number of eligible adults in the household to compensate for unequal, household selection probabilities. The 1992 and 1996 data are weighted to compensate for unequal probabilities of selection for respondents in different size households and for differential nonresponse across geographic sample design categories and between panel and cross-section respondents. The 1992 weight also post-stratifies the sample to 1990 Census proportions for 24 age by sex by census region categories. The 1996 weight post-stratifies to the July 1995 Census population projections for age, by sex by Census region categories. The descriptions for these weights and advice concerning their use were taken from the NES codebooks for each set of data. The weights are described as follows: 1988 (mean = 1.83, SD = 0.76, min = 1, max = 6, 57 >= 3, 169 = 3, 952 = 2, 594 = 1), 1992 (mean = 0.9987, SD = 0.368, min = 0.4564, max = 1.7249), 1996 (mean = 0.9999, SD = 0.541, min = 0.3436, max = 3.4278).

[79] Several of the variables included in this model may be endogenous to political participation. That is, measures of efficacy or political knowledge

taken after the political activity occurred may be affected by the activity itself. The result would be biased parameter estimates. Excluding variables that have been shown to affect participation would also yield biased and incorrect estimates for some of the remaining variables. Because the relative effect of age, a variable clearly exogenous to participation or mobilization, is the emphasis of this analysis I report the full model. Any biases in this estimate will be consistent across the three models and as a result the comparison of the effects should be legitimate. Further analysis of this model would correct for these weaknesses. Additionally, the model may be affected by a slight level of collinearity among the independent variables that would inflate the standard errors. The highest correlation with age among the three elections is 0.5 with employment.

[80]   Voter turnout percentages are likely inflated due to individuals' desire to give socially-desirable responses to particular questions. To provide more accurate information, the sponsors of the NES occasionally conduct voter validation studies. The validation study of 1988 was not used for this analysis because there is no corresponding correction for 1992 or 1996. Also, validation introduces other errors and does not significantly increase the reliability of the data (Belli et al. 1994). Finally, the voter validation study of 1988 was used to examine the characteristics of the 214 people who reported voting and were then found to have not voted. While these respondents were slightly more likely to be younger, shifting them to the nonvote category did not change significantly the results for 1988. Accordingly, no adjustment was made for 1992 or 1996 to account for overreporting of voter turnout.

[81]   "Americans" refers to the adults interviewed for this survey. Because this is a sample subject to error, the adults surveyed may not represent all Americans. However, based on the sampling procedures, the sample size, and the quality of the instrument, which are designed to reduce sources of error, I am confident that the responses are a reasonable representation of the responses of the American public in the coterminous United States.

[82]   The percentage for older Americans is subtracted from the percentage for younger Americans.

[83]   Beginning with a key, the Appendix for Chapter Three contains the full model for each table.

[84]   Tables for each full model are included in the Appendix.

CHAPTER FOUR

Conclusion

Medicare is an overwhelmingly popular program with the American public. While many Americans accepted that Medicare had to be reformed in 1995 to avoid bankruptcy, most Americans were not willing to support major changes or changes that would have increased the burden on Medicare recipients. The public's opposition to the 1995 proposals to reform Medicare was used to help explain why the Republican majority in the House of Representatives loss seats in the 1996 election. Additionally, in this project, older Americans' views on Medicare reform were used to explain their increased political participation in the 1996 election. Thus, policymakers who advocate major reform of Medicare must somehow shift the public's attitudes concerning acceptable changes to the program.

Based on the results of the first two studies included in this project, neither critical media coverage of policymakers nor knowledge of the Medicare program had a significant impact on the public's support for policymakers reforming the program or specific policy proposals. A closer examination of the tables in the Appendix for Chapter Two reveals that no one socio-economic or political variable predicts support for Medicare across the range of policy reforms proposed in 1995. So, although Medicare faces financing and other policy dilemmas, the lack of public support ensures that major reform is unlikely in the near future without a better understanding of what explains the likelihood of support for Medicare policy and a major effort to change the public's views, or a major change in outlook for Medicare beneficiaries or the Medicare program.

Appendix For Chapter Two

Table A1: Descriptive Statistics, n=1,383

Independent Variables		% of Respondents category
Medicare Knowledge Index each category is number of correct responses	0	*
	1	3
	2	8
	3	20
	4	30
	5	26
	6	10
	7	2
Age		
	18-29	24
	30-49	42
	50-64	12
	65+	22
	Not Sure	*
Regardless of how you might vote, what do you usually consider yourself - a Republican, a Democrat, and Independent, or what?	Rep	32
	Other	2
	Ind	29
	Dem	34
	Not sure	2
How would you describe your own political philosophy - conserv-ative, moderate, and liberal?	Consv.	40
	Mod.	38
	Liberal	18
	Not sure	3
Race	White	80
	African-American	12
	Asian	1
	Indian	1
	Other	3
	Not sure	1

Table A2: Descriptive Statistics, n=1,383

Independent Variables	% of Respondents category	
Total 1994 household income	< = 7.5 k	9
	7.501-15k	11
	15.001-25k	18
	25.001-35k	16
	35.001-50k	17
	50.001-75k	14
	75.001-100k	4
	100.001k +	4
	Not sure	6
Education	< H.S.	12
	HS grad/equiv.	42
	Some collg.	26
	Collg. grad.	14
	Post grd	6
	Not sure/refused	*
Sex	Male	48
	Female	52

Table A5: Probit Parameter Estimates for Likelihood of Favoring Moving Beneficiaries from Free-for-Service to Managed Care (Full Index)

	Model Without Knowledge Variable Log Likelihood= -817.31 n=1343			Model With Knowledge Variable Log Likelihood= -814.25 n=1343		
	Para-meter Est.	Rob. SE	DY/ Dx	Para-meter Est.	Rob. SE	DY/ Dx
Intercept	0.00	0.13	--	0.04	0.13	--
Full Knowledge Index	--	--	--	0.15	0.09	0.06
Age 18-49 (ref)						
Age 50-64	-0.18	0.13	-0.07	-0.19	0.13	-0.07
Age 65+	-0.80	0.10	-0.26	-0.82	0.10	-0.27
Republican party (ref)						
Democrat	-0.46	0.11	-0.16	-0.47	0.11	-0.17
Independent/Other	-0.27	0.11	-0.10	-0.27	0.11	-0.10
Conservative ideology (ref)						
Moderate	-0.09	0.10	-0.03	-0.09	0.10	-0.03
Liberal	-0.33	0.13	-0.12	-0.32	0.13	-0.11
White Race (ref)						
African-American	0.10	0.15	0.04	0.12	0.15	0.05
Asian/other	0.03	0.20	0.01	0.04	0.20	0.02
Income <= $25,000 (ref)						
Income $25,000-$50,000	0.09	0.11	0.04	0.08	0.11	0.03
Income >=$50,001	0.33	0.12	0.12	0.31	0.12	0.12
H.S deg./equiv. or less (ref)						
Some College	0.03	0.10	0.01	0.04	0.10	0.01
College/post. graduate degree	-0.00	0.11	-0.00	-0.01	0.11	-0.00
Female (ref)						
Male	0.04	0.09	0.02	0.05	0.09	0.02
Model X^2	131			134		

Notes: 1) Model calculated using robust standard errors. 2) DY/Dx designates how much the independent variable being true changes the outcome probability over that of the independent variable being false. 3) Model X^2 tests for the overall fit of the model. 4) Bold estimates significant at $p < 0.05$; italicized estimates significant at $p < 0.10$.

Table A4: Probit Parameter Estimates for Likelihood of Favoring A Voucher System for Medicare
(Benefits Index)

	Model Without Knowledge Variable Log Likelihood= -816.31 n=1343			Model With Knowledge Variable Log Likelihood= -816.14 n=1343		
	Para- meter Est.	Rob. SE	DY/ Dx	Para- meter Est.	Rob. SE	DY/ Dx
Intercept	0.00	0.13	--	0.02	0.14	--
Full Knowledge Index	--	--	--	-0.04	0.09	-0.02
Age 18-49 (ref)						
Age 50-64	-0.18	0.13	-0.07	-0.18	0.13	-0.06
Age 65+	*-0.80*	*0.10*	*-0.26*	*-0.79*	*0.10*	*-0.26*
Republican party (ref)						
Democrat	**-0.46**	**0.11**	**-0.16**	**-0.46**	**0.11**	**-0.16**
Independent/Other	*-0.27*	*0.11*	*-0.10*	**-0.26**	**0.11**	**-0.10**
Conservative ideology (ref)						
Moderate	-0.09	0.10	-0.03	-0.09	0.10	-0.04
Liberal	**-0.33**	**0.13**	**-0.12**	**-0.33**	**0.13**	**-0.12**
White Race (ref)						
African-American	0.10	0.15	0.04	0.10	0.15	0.04
Asian/other	0.03	0.20	0.01	0.02	0.20	0.01
Income <= $25,000 (ref)						
Income $25,000-$50,000	0.09	0.11	0.04	0.10	0.11	0.04
Income >=$50,001	**0.33**	**0.12**	**0.12**	**0.33**	**0.12**	**0.12**
H.S deg./equiv. or less (ref)						
Some College	0.03	0.10	0.01	0.03	0.10	0.01
College/post. graduate degree	-0.00	0.11	-0.00	-0.00	0.11	0.00
Female (ref)						
Male	0.04	0.09	0.02	0.04	0.09	0.02

Model X^2 131   132

Notes: 1) Model calculated using robust standard errors. 2) DY/Dx designates how much the independent variable being true changes the outcome probability over that of the independent variable being false. 3) Model X^2 tests for the overall fit of the model. 4) Bold estimates significant at $p < 0.05$; italicized estimates significant at $p < 0.10$.

Table A5: Probit Parameter Estimates for Likelihood of Favoring Moving Beneficiaries from Fee-for-Service to Managed Care (Full Index)

	Model Without Knowledge Variable Log Likelihood= -867.85 n=1347			Model With Knowledge Variable Log Likelihood= -866.58 n=1347		
	Para-meter Est.	Rob. SE	DY/ Dx	Para-meter Est.	Rob. SE	DY/ Dx
Intercept	-0.19	0.12	--	-0.23	0.13	--
Full Knowledge Index	--	--	--	0.12	0.09	0.05
Age 18-49 (ref)						
Age 50-64	-0.36	0.13	-0.14	-0.37	0.13	-0.15
Age 65+	-0.67	0.10	-0.29	-0.68	0.10	-0.26
Republican party (ref)						
Democrat	0.22	0.11	0.09	0.22	0.11	0.09
Independent/Other	0.14	0.10	0.06	0.14	0.10	0.05
Conservative ideology (ref)						
Moderate	-0.00	0.10	-0.00	0.00	0.10	-0.00
Liberal	*-0.10*	0.13	*-0.04*	*-0.10*	0.13	*-0.04*
White Race (ref)						
African-American	-0.30	0.15	-0.12	-0.28	0.15	-0.11
Asian/other	-0.05	0.20	-0.02	-0.04	0.20	-0.02
Income <= $25,000 (ref)						
Income $25,000-$50,000	0.26	0.10	0.10	0.25	0.10	0.10
Income >=$50,001	0.44	0.12	0.17	0.43	0.12	0.17
H.S deg./equiv. or less (ref)						
Some College	-0.00	0.10	-0.00	-0.00	0.10	-0.00
College/post. graduate degree	*0.19*	0.10	*0.08*	*0.18*	0.10	*0.07*
Female (ref)						
Male	0.19	0.08	0.08	0.20	0.09	0.08
Model X^2	118			120		

Notes: 1) Model calculated using robust standard errors. 2) DY/Dx designates how much the independent variable being true changes the outcome probability over that of the independent variable being false. 3) Model X^2 tests for the overall fit of the model. 4) Bold estimates significant at $p < 0.05$; italicized estimates significant at $p < 0.10$.

Table A6: Probit Parameter Estimates for Likelihood of Favoring Moving Beneficiaries from Fee-for-Service to Managed Care(Benefits Index)

	Model Without Knowledge Variable Log Likelihood= -867.85 n=1347			Model With Knowledge Variable Log Likelihood= -866.66 n=1347		
	Para-meter Est.	Rob. SE	DY/Dx	Para-meter Est.	Rob. SE	DY/Dx
Intercept	-0.19	0.12	--	-0.17	0.13	--
Full Knowledge Index	--	--	--	-0.04	0.09	-0.02
Age 18-49 (ref)						
Age 50-64	-0.36	0.13	-0.14	-0.36	0.13	-0.14
Age 65+	-0.67	0.10	-0.29	-0.66	0.10	-0.25
Republican party (ref)						
Democrat	0.22	0.11	-0.09	-0.22	0.11	0.09
Independent/Other	0.14	0.10	-0.06	0.14	0.10	0.06
Conservative ideology (ref)						
Moderate	-0.00	0.10	-0.00	-0.00	0.10	-0.00
Liberal	-0.10	0.13	-0.04	-0.10	0.12	-0.04
White Race (ref)						
African-American	-0.30	0.15	-0.12	-0.30	0.15	-0.12
Asian/other	-0.05	0.20	-0.02	-0.06	0.20	-0.02
Income <= $25,000 (ref)						
Income $25,000-$50,000	0.26	0.10	0.10	0.26	0.10	0.10
Income >=$50,001	0.44	0.12	0.17	0.45	0.12	0.18
H.S deg./equiv. or less (ref)						
Some College	-0.00	0.10	-0.00	-0.00	0.10	-0.00
College/post. graduate degree	0.19	0.10	0.08	0.20	0.10	0.08
Female (ref)						
Male	0.19	0.08	0.08	0.19	0.08	0.08
Model X^2	118			119		

Notes: 1) Model calculated using robust standard errors. 2) DY/Dx designates how much the independent variable being true changes the outcome probability over that of the independent variable being false. 3) Model X^2 tests for the overall fit of the model. 4) Bold estimates significant at p < 0.05; italicized estimates significant at p < 0.10.

Table A7: Probit Parameter Estimates for Likelihood of Favoring an Increase in the Payroll Tax to Address Medicare's Issues (Full Index)

	Model Without Knowledge Variable Log Likelihood= -783.08 n=1326			Model With Knowledge Variable Log Likelihood= -782.60 n=1326		
	Para-meter Est.	Rob. SE	DY/ Dx	Para-meter Est.	Rob. SE	DY/ Dx
Intercept	**-0.89**	0.14	--	**-0.92**	0.14	--
Full Knowledge Index	--	--	--	0.08	0.09	0.03
Age 18-49 (ref)						
Age 50-64	0.16	0.14	0.06	0.16	0.14	0.06
Age 65+	**0.34**	0.10	**0.12**	**0.33**	0.10	**0.12**
Republican party (ref)						
Democrat	**-0.22**	0.11	**0.11**	**-0.31**	0.11	**0.11**
Independent/Other	**-0.14**	0.10	0.05	0.14	0.11	0.05
Conservative ideology (ref)						
Moderate	0.07	0.10	0.02	0.08	0.10	0.03
Liberal	0.05	0.13	0.02	0.05	0.13	0.02
White Race (ref)						
African-American	0.12	0.15	0.04	0.14	0.15	0.05
Asian/other	0.25	0.20	0.09	0.27	0.20	0.10
Income <= $25,000 (ref)						
Income $25,000-$50,000	0.12	0.10	0.04	0.11	0.10	0.04
Income >=$50,001	0.10	0.13	0.04	0.10	0.13	0.03
H.S deg./equiv. or less (ref)						
Some College	**-0.26**	0.11	**-0.09**	**-0.26**	0.11	**-0.08**
College/post. graduate degree	0.00	0.11	0.00	0.00	0.11	-0.00
Female (ref)						
Male	0.08	0.09	*0.03*	0.08	0.09	0.03

Model X^2 33.7   34.0

Notes: 1) Model calculated using robust standard errors. 2) DY/Dx designates how much the independent variable being true changes the outcome probability over that of the independent variable being false. 3) Model X^2 tests for the overall fit of the model. 4) Bold estimates significant at p < 0.05; italicized estimates significant at p < 0.10.

Table A8: Probit Parameter Estimates for Likelihood of Favoring an Increase in the Payroll Tax to Address Medicare's Issues (Benefits Index)

	Model Without Knowledge Variable Log Likelihood= -783.08 n=1326			Model With Knowledge Variable Log Likelihood= -783.08 n=1326		
	Para-meter Est.	Rob. SE	DY/Dx	Para-meter Est.	Rob. SE	DY/Dx
Intercept	**-0.89**	0.14	--	**-0.90**	0.15	--
Full Knowledge Index	--	--	--	0.01	0.09	0.00
Age 18-49 (ref)						
Age 50-64	0.16	0.14	0.06	0.16	0.14	0.06
Age 65+	**0.34**	0.10	**0.12**	**0.34**	0.10	**0.12**
Republican party (ref)						
Democrat	**0.31**	0.11	**0.11**	**-0.31**	0.11	**0.11**
Independent/Other	0.14	0.11	0.05	0.14	0.11	0.05
Conservative ideology (ref)						
Moderate	0.07	0.10	0.02	0.07	0.10	0.02
Liberal	0.05	0.13	0.02	0.05	0.13	0.02
White Race (ref)						
African-American	0.12	0.15	0.04	0.12	0.14	0.04
Asian/other	0.25	0.20	0.09	0.26	0.20	0.09
Income <= $25,000 (ref)						
Income $25,000-$50,000	0.12	0.10	0.04	0.12	0.10	0.04
Income >=$50,001	0.10	0.13	0.04	0.10	0.13	0.034
H.S deg./equiv. or less (ref)						
Some College	**-0.26**	0.11	**-0.09**	**-0.26**	0.11	**-0.08**
College/post. graduate degree	0.00	0.11	0.00	0.00	0.11	-0.00
Female (ref)						
Male	0.08	0.09	**0.03**	0.08	0.09	0.03

Model X^2 33.7   33.7

Notes: 1) Model calculated using robust standard errors. 2) DY/Dx designates how much the independent variable being true changes the outcome probability over that of the independent variable being false. 3) Model X^2 tests for the overall fit of the model. 4) Bold estimates significant at p < 0.05; italicized estimates significant at p < 0.10.

Table A9: Probit Parameter Estimates for Likelihood of Favoring Increasing the Age of Eligibility from 65 to 67 in the Year 2000 to Address Medicare's Issues (Full Index)

	Model Without Knowledge Variable Log Likelihood= -870.78 n=1358			Model With Knowledge Variable Log Likelihood= -869.60 n=1358		
	Para-meter Est.	Rob. SE	DY/ Dx	Para-meter Est.	Rob. SE	DY/ Dx
Intercept	-0.35	0.12	--	-0.38	0.13	--
Full Knowledge Index	--	--	--	0.11	0.08	0.04
Age 18-49 (ref)						
Age 50-64	0.14	0.13	0.06	0.13	0.13	0.05
Age 65+	0.57	0.09	0.22	0.56	0.09	0.22
Republican party (ref)						
Democrat	-0.20	0.11	-0.08	-0.20	0.11	-0.08
Independent/Other	-0.01	0.10	-0.00	-0.01	0.10	-0.00
Conservative ideology (ref)						
Moderate	-0.16	0.10	-0.06	-0.15	0.10	-0.06
Liberal	-0.22	0.13	-0.08	-0.21	0.13	-0.08
White Race (ref)						
African-American	-0.26	0.16	-0.10	-0.24	0.16	-0.09
Asian/other	-0.26	0.20	-0.10	-0.24	0.20	-0.09
Income <= $25,000 (ref)						
Income $25,000-$50,000	0.03	0.10	0.01	0.02	0.10	0.01
Income >=$50,001	0.14	0.12	0.06	0.13	0.12	0.05
H.S deg./equiv. or less (ref)						
Some College	0.36	0.10	0.14	0.36	0.10	0.14
College/post. graduate degree	0.42	0.10	0.16	0.41	0.10	0.16
Female (ref)						
Male	-0.05	0.08	-0.02	-0.04	0.08	-0.02

Model X^2	75.0	76.0

Notes: 1) Model calculated using robust standard errors. 2) DY/Dx designates how much the independent variable being true changes the outcome probability over that of the independent variable being false. 3) Model X^2 tests for the overall fit of the model. 4) Bold estimates significant at $p < 0.05$; italicized estimates significant at $p < 0.10$.

Table A10: Probit Parameter Estimates for Likelihood of Favoring Increasing the Age of Eligibility from 65 to 67 in the Year 2000 to Address Medicare's Issues (Benefits Index)

	Model Without Knowledge Variable Log Likelihood= -870.78 n=1358			Model With Knowledge Variable Log Likelihood= -868.62 n=1358		
	Para-meter Est.	Rob. SE	DY/ Dx	Para-meter Est.	Rob. SE	DY/ Dx
Intercept	-0.35	0.12	--	-0.27	0.13	--
Full Knowledge Index	--	--	--	-0.15	0.09	-0.06
Age 18-49 (ref)						
Age 50-64	0.14	0.13	0.06	0.15	0.13	0.06
Age 65+	0.57	0.09	0.22	0.60	0.10	0.24
Republican party (ref)						
Democrat	-0.20	0.11	-0.08	-0.19	0.11	-0.07
Independent/Other	-0.01	0.10	-0.00	-0.00	0.10	-0.00
Conservative ideology (ref)						
Moderate	-0.16	0.10	-0.06	-0.16	0.10	-0.06
Liberal	-0.22	0.13	-0.08	-0.22	0.12	-0.08
White Race (ref)						
African-American	-0.26	0.16	-0.10	-0.27	0.15	-0.10
Asian/other	-0.26	0.20	-0.10	-0.29	0.20	-0.11
Income <= $25,000 (ref)						
Income $25,000-$50,000	0.03	0.10	0.01	0.03	0.10	0.01
Income >=$50,001	0.14	0.12	0.06	0.14	0.12	0.06
H.S deg./equiv. or less (ref)						
Some College	0.36	0.10	0.14	0.37	0.10	0.14
College/post. graduate degree	0.42	0.10	0.16	0.43	0.10	0.17
Female (ref)						
Male	-0.05	0.08	-0.02	-0.05	0.08	-0.02
Model X^2	75.0			81.4		

Notes: 1) Model calculated using robust standard errors. 2) DY/Dx designates how much the independent variable being true changes the outcome probability over that of the independent variable being false. 3) Model X^2 tests for the overall fit of the model. 4) Bold estimates significant at $p < 0.05$; italicized estimates significant at $p < 0.10$.

Table A11: Probit Parameter Estimates for Favoring a Reduction in Benefits to Medicare Recipients to Address Medicare's Issues (Full Index)

	Model Without Knowledge Variable Log Likelihood= --618.11 n=1343			Model With Knowledge Variable Log Likelihood= -617.07 n=1343		
	Para-meter Est.	Rob. SE	DY/Dx	Para-meter Est.	Rob. SE	DY/Dx
Intercept	-0.91	0.14	--	-0.87	0.15	--
Full Knowledge Index	--	--	--	-0.12	0.10	-0.03
Age 18-49 (ref)						
Age 50-64	-0.29	0.16	-0.07	-0.27	0.16	-0.06
Age 65+	-0.06	0.11	-0.01	-0.04	0.11	-0.01
Republican party (ref)						
Democrat	-0.33	0.13	-0.08	-0.32	0.13	-0.08
Independent/Other	-0.18	0.12	-0.04	-0.18	0.12	-0.04
Conservative ideology (ref)						
Moderate	-0.20	0.11	-0.05	-0.20	0.11	-0.05
Liberal	-0.24	0.15	-0.06	-0.25	0.15	-0.06
White Race (ref)						
African-American	0.39	0.16	0.11	0.37	0.16	0.11
Asian/other	0.11	0.21	0.03	0.11	0.21	0.03
Income <= $25,000 (ref)						
Income $25,000-$50,000	0.19	0.12	0.05	0.20	0.12	0.05
Income >=$50,001	0.19	0.14	0.05	0.20	0.14	0.06
H.S deg./equiv. or less (ref)						
Some College	-0.17	0.12	-0.04	-0.16	0.12	-0.04
College/post. graduate degree	0.12	0.12	0.03	0.14	0.12	0.04
Female (ref)						
Male	0.33	0.10	0.08	0.33	0.10	0.08
Model X^2	43.7			46.8		

Notes: 1) Model calculated using robust standard errors. 2) DY/Dx designates how much the independent variable being true changes the outcome probability over that of the independent variable being false. 3) Model X^2 tests for the overall fit of the model. 4) Bold estimates significant at $p < 0.05$; italicized estimates significant at $p < 0.10$.

Table A12: Probit Parameter Estimates for Favoring a Reduction in Benefits to Medicare Recipients to Address Medicare's Issues (Benefits Index)

	Model Without Knowledge Variable Log Likelihood= -618.11 n=1343			Model With Knowledge Variable Log Likelihood= -615.07 n=1343		
	Para-meter Est.	Rob. SE	DY/ Dx	Para-meter Est.	Rob. SE	DY/ Dx
Intercept	-0.91	0.14	--	-0.81	0.15	--
Full Knowledge Index	--	--	--	-0.21	0.10	-0.05
Age 18-49 (ref)						
Age 50-64	-0.29	0.16	-0.07	-0.28	0.16	-0.06
Age 65+	-0.06	0.11	-0.01	-0.01	0.11	-0.00
Republican party (ref)						
Democrat	-0.33	0.13	-0.08	-0.32	0.13	-0.08
Independent/Other	-0.18	0.12	-0.04	-0.17	0.12	-0.04
Conservative ideology (ref)						
Moderate	-0.20	0.11	-0.05	-0.20	0.11	-0.05
Liberal	-0.24	0.15	-0.06	-0.24	0.15	-0.06
White Race (ref)						
African-American	0.39	0.16	0.11	0.37	0.16	0.11
Asian/other	0.11	0.21	0.03	0.07	0.21	0.02
Income <= $25,000 (ref)						
Income $25,000-$50,000	0.19	0.12	0.05	0.19	0.12	0.05
Income >=$50,001	0.19	0.14	0.05	0.19	0.14	0.05
H.S deg./equiv. or less (ref)						
Some College	-0.17	0.12	-0.04	-0.15	0.12	-0.04
College/post. graduate degree	0.12	0.12	0.03	0.14	0.12	0.04
Female (ref)						
Male	0.33	0.10	0.08	0.32	0.10	0.08

Model X^2 43.7   50.1

Notes: 1) Model calculated using robust standard errors. 2) DY/Dx designates how much the independent variable being true changes the outcome probability over that of the independent variable being false. 3) Model X^2 tests for the overall fit of the model. 4) Bold estimates significant at p < 0.05; italicized estimates significant at p < 0.10.

Table A13: Probit Parameter Estimates for Likelihood of Favoring an Increase in Premiums to Address Medicare's Issues (Full Index)

	Model Without Knowledge Variable Log Likelihood= -823.84 n=1337			Model With Knowledge Variable Log Likelihood= -812.64 n=1337		
	Para- meter Est.	Rob. SE	DY/ Dx	Para- meter Est.	Rob. SE	DY/ Dx
Intercept	-0.50	0.13	--	-0.44	0.13	--
Full Knowledge Index	--	--	--	-0.21	0.09	-0.08
Age 18-49 (ref)						
Age 50-64	-0.05	0.14	-0.02	-0.04	0.14	-0.01
Age 65+	0.32	0.10	0.12	0.35	0.10	0.13
Republican party (ref)						
Democrat	-0.25	0.11	-0.09	-0.24	0.11	-0.08
Independent/Other	-0.17	0.10	-0.06	-0.18	0.10	-0.06
Conservative ideology (ref)						
Moderate	0.03	0.10	0.01	0.03	0.10	0.01
Liberal	-0.08	0.13	-0.03	-0.10	0.13	-0.04
White Race (ref)						
African-American	-0.10	0.16	-0.04	-0.13	0.16	-0.05
Asian/other	0.17	0.20	0.06	0.14	0.20	0.05
Income <= $25,000 (ref)						
Income $25,000-$50,000	-0.06	0.10	-0.02	-0.05	0.10	-0.02
Income >=$50,001	0.16	0.12	0.06	0.18	0.12	0.07
H.S deg./equiv. or less (ref)						
Some College	0.08	0.10	0.03	0.08	0.10	-0.03
College/post. graduate degree	0.38	0.10	0.14	0.40	0.10	0.15
Female (ref)						
Male	0.07	0.09	0.02	0.06	0.09	0.02
Model X^2	42.1			49.1		

Notes: 1) Model calculated using robust standard errors. 2) DY/Dx designates how much the independent variable being true changes the outcome probability over that of the independent variable being false. 3) Model X^2 tests for the overall fit of the model. 4) Bold estimates significant at $p < 0.05$; italicized estimates significant at $p < 0.10$.

Table A14: Probit Parameter Estimates for Likelihood of Favoring an Increase in Premiums to Address Medicare's Issues (Benefits Index)

	Model Without Knowledge Variable Log Likelihood= -823.84 n=1337			Model With Knowledge Variable Log Likelihood= -817.94 n=1337		
	Para-meter Est.	Rob. SE	DY/ Dx	Para-meter Est.	Rob. SE	DY/ Dx
Intercept	-0.50	0.13	--	-0.39	0.13	--
Full Knowledge Index	--	--	--	-0.26	0.09	-0.09
Age 18-49 (ref)						
Age 50-64	-0.05	0.14	-0.02	0.04	0.14	-0.01
Age 65+	0.32	0.10	0.12	0.39	0.10	0.14
Republican party (ref)						
Democrat	-0.25	0.11	-0.09	-0.24	0.11	-0.08
Independent/Other	-0.17	0.10	-0.06	-0.18	0.10	-0.06
Conservative ideology (ref)						
Moderate	0.03	0.10	0.01	0.03	0.10	0.01
Liberal	-0.08	0.13	-0.03	-0.08	0.13	-0.03
White Race (ref)						
African-American	-0.10	0.16	-0.04	-0.13	0.16	-0.04
Asian/other	0.17	0.20	0.06	0.12	0.20	0.04
Income <= $25,000 (ref)						
Income $25,000-$50,000	-0.06	0.10	-0.02	-0.09	0.10	-0.02
Income >=$50,001	0.16	0.12	0.06	0.16	0.12	0.06
H.S deg./equiv. or less (ref)						
Some College	0.08	0.10	0.03	0.08	0.10	-0.03
College/post. graduate degree	0.38	0.10	0.14	0.40	0.10	0.15
Female (ref)						
Male	0.07	0.09	0.02	0.06	0.09	0.02

Model X^2 42.1   51.0

Notes: 1) Model calculated using robust standard errors. 2) DY/Dx designates how much the independent variable being true changes the outcome probability over that of the independent variable being false. 3) Model X^2 tests for the overall fit of the model. 4) Bold estimates significant at $p < 0.05$; italicized estimates significant at $p < 0.10$.

Table A15: Probit Parameter Estimates for Likelihood of Favoring A Voucher System for Medicare, n = 1,343

	Full Information Index Log Likelihood = -804.78			Benefits Information Index Log Likelihood = -802.26		
	Parameter Estimate	Parameter Est. for Interaction: Know*X_i	DY/Dx for Interaction	Parameter Estimate	Parameter Est. for Interaction: Know*X_i	DY/Dx for Interaction
Intercept	-0.15 (0.16)	--	--	-0.09 (0.20)	--	--
Less Well-Informed (ref)						
Well-informed	0.44 (0.26)	--	--	0.16 (0.26)	--	--
Age 18-49 (ref)						
Age 50-64	0.00 (0.17)	-0.47 (0.27)	0.16	-0.17 (0.20)	0.02 (0.27)	0.00
Age 65+	-0.88 (0.13)	0.10 (0.20)	0.04	-0.56 (0.17)	-0.30 (0.21)	-0.11
Republican Party (ref)						
Democrat	-0.47 (0.15)	0.02 (0.23)	0.01	-0.70 (0.18)	0.40 (0.23)	0.15
Independent/Other	-0.31 (0.14)	0.15 (0.22)	0.06	-0.43 (0.16)	0.30 (0.22)	0.15
Conservative ideology (ref)						
Moderate	-0.06 (0.13)	-0.11 (0.20)	-0.04	0.13 (0.15)	-0.41 (0.20)	-0.14
Liberal	-0.23 (0.17)	-0.23 (0.28)	-0.08	-0.25 (0.21)	-0.13 (0.27)	-0.05
White race (ref)						
African-American	0.01 (0.18)	0.42 (0.34)	0.16	0.10 (0.22)	0.02 (0.30)	0.00
Asian/other	-0.10 (0.23)	0.58 (0.43)	0.23	-0.24 (0.25)	0.81 (0.42)	0.32
Income < = $25,000 (ref)						
Income $25,001-$50,000	0.15 (0.14)	-0.19 (0.22)	-0.07	0.01 (0.17)	0.15 (0.22)	0.06
Income >=$50,001	0.26 (0.16)	0.13 (0.26)	0.05	0.32 (0.19)	0.04 (0.25)	0.02
H.S. deg./equiv. or less (ref)						
some college	0.14 (0.13)	-0.34 (0.22)	-0.12	0.21 (0.16)	-0.33 (0.21)	-0.11
College/post. graduate deg.	0.09 (0.14)	-0.28 (0.22)	-0.10	0.17 (0.17)	-0.27 (0.22)	-0.10
Female (ref)						
Male	0.12 (0.11)	-0.20 (0.18)	-0.07	0.22 (0.14)	0.39 (0.18)	-0.14
Model χ^2	151			152		

Notes: 1) Model calculated using robust standard errors. 2) Standard errors of parameter estimates are in parantheses. 3) Model χ^2 tests for the overall fit of the model. 4) The interaction term is the knowledge Index (coded 0,1) multiplied by each independent variable (coded 0,1). 5) DY/Dx designates how much the independent variable being true changes the outcome probability over that of the independent variable being false. 6) Bold estimates significant at p < 0.10.

Table A16: Probit Parameter Estimates for Likelihood of Favoring Moving Beneficiaries from Fee-for-Service to Managed Care, n= 1,347

	Full Information Index Log Likelihood = -863.14			Benefits Information Index Log Likelihood = -861.09		
	Parameter Estimate	Parameter Est. for Inter-action: Know*X_i	DY/Dx for Inter-action	Parameter Estimate	Parameter Est. for Inter-action: Know*X_i	DY/Dx for Inter-action
Intercept	**-0.28** (0.16)	--	--	**-0.23** (0.19)	--	--
Less Well-Informed (ref) Well-informed	0.28 (0.26)	--	--	0.08 (0.25)	--	--
Age 18-49 (ref) Age 50-64	**-0.33** (0.17)	-0.08 (0.26)	-0.03	**-0.48** (0.19)	0.21 (0.26)	0.08
Age 65+	**-0.68** (0.13)	-0.02 (0.20)	-0.01	**-0.36** (0.17)	**-0.43** (0.21)	**-0.17**
Republican Party (ref) Democrat	0.19 (0.14)	0.08 (0.23)	0.03	0.14 (0.17)	0.12 (0.22)	0.05
Independent/Other	0.17 (0.13)	-0.09 (0.22)	-0.04	0.11 (0.16)	0.04 (0.22)	0.02
Conservative ideology (ref) Moderate	-0.02 (0.12)	0.09 (0.20)	0.03	0.05 (0.15)	-0.10 (0.20)	-0.04
Liberal	-0.06 (0.16)	-0.14 (0.27)	-0.06	0.04 (0.20)	-0.26 (0.26)	-0.10
White race (ref) African-American	-0.24 (0.17)	-0.17 (0.35)	-0.07	*0.38* (0.21)	0.16 (0.29)	0.06
Asian/other	-0.06 (0.24)	0.02 (0.45)	0.01	-0.13 (0.26)	0.23 (0.42)	0.09
Income < = $25,000 (ref) Income $25,001-$50,000	*0.22* (0.13)	0.05 (0.21)	0.02	0.19 (0.16)	0.13 (0.20)	0.05
Income >=$50,001	**0.55** (0.16)	-0.30 (0.25)	-0.12	*0.56* (0.19)	-0.18 (0.25)	-0.07
H.S. deg./equiv. or less (ref) some college	0.03 (0.13)	-0.12 (0.21)	-0.05	0.11 (0.16)	-0.21 (0.21)	-0.08
College/post. graduate deg.	0.19 (0.14)	-0.01 (0.21)	-0.00	0.17 (0.17)	-0.09 (0.21)	-0.03
Female (ref) Male	*0.24* (0.11)	-0.11 (0.18)	-0.04	*0.24* (0.14)	-0.09 (0.18)	-0.04
Model χ^2	**129**			**134**		

Notes: 1) Model calculated using robust standard errors. 2) Standard errors of parameter estimates are in parantheses. 3) Model χ^2 tests for the overall fit of the model. 4) The interaction term is the knowledge Index (coded 0,1) multiplied by each independent variable (coded 0,1). 5) DY/Dx designates how much the independent variable being true changes the outcome probability over that of the independent variable being false. 6) Bold estimates significant at p < 0.10.

Table A17: Probit Parameter Estimates for Likelihood of Favoring An Increase in the Payroll Tax to Address Medicare's Issues, n = 1,326

	Full Information Index Log Likelihood = -777.50			Benefits Information Index Log Likelihood = -769.34		
	Parameter Estimate	Parameter Est. for Inter- action: Know*X_i	DY/Dx for Inter- action	Parameter Estimate	Parameter Est. for Inter- action: Know*X_i	DY/Dx for Inter- action
Intercept	-0.93 (0.17)	--	--	-0.79 (0.22)	--	--
Less Well-Informed (ref) Well-informed	0.12 (0.29)	--	--	-0.22 (0.28)	--	--
Age 18-49 (ref) Age 50-64	0.23 (0.18)	-0.18 (0.27)	-0.06	0.14 (0.21)	0.02 (0.28)	0.01
Age 65+	0.32 (0.13)	0.01 (0.20)	0.00	0.54 (0.18)	-0.31 (0.21)	-0.10
Republican Party (ref) Democrat	0.23 (0.15)	0.19 (0.23)	0.07	0.08 (0.18)	0.40 (0.23)	0.14
Independent/Other	0.07 (0.15)	0.16 (0.23)	0.06	0.17 (0.18)	-0.03 (0.23)	-0.01
Conservative ideology (ref) Moderate	0.10 (0.13)	-0.05 (0.21)	-0.02	0.15 (0.16)	-0.14 (0.21)	-0.04
Liberal	0.08 (0.16)	-0.08 (0.27)	-0.03	0.36 (0.20)	-0.61 (0.26)	-0.18
White race (ref) African-American	0.27 (0.17)	-0.52 (0.34)	-0.15	0.17 (0.21)	-0.09 (0.30)	-0.03
Asian/other	0.28 (0.24)	0.08 (0.43)	-0.03	0.19 (0.26)	0.16 (0.42)	0.05
Income < = $25,000 (ref) Income $25,001-$50,000	0.04 (0.14)	0.18 (0.22)	0.06	-0.05 (0.17)	0.28 (0.22)	0.10
Income >=$50,001	0.17 (0.16)	0.18 (0.26)	-0.06	0.15 (0.19)	-0.03 (0.26)	-0.01
H.S. deg./equiv. or less (ref) some college	-0.20 (0.14)	-0.17 (0.22)	-0.06	-0.29 (0.17)	0.04 (0.22)	0.01
College/post. graduate deg.	0.11 (0.14)	-0.23 (0.22)	-0.07	-0.32 (0.17)	0.55 (0.22)	0.20
Female (ref) Male	0.07 (0.12)	0.02 (0.18)	0.01	-0.02 (0.14)	0.21 (0.19)	0.07
Model χ^2	41.2			59.9		

Notes: 1) Model calculated using robust standard errors. 2) Standard errors of parameter estimates are in parantheses. 3) Model χ^2 tests for the overall fit of the model. 4) The interaction term is the knowledge Index (coded 0,1) multiplied by each independent variable (coded 0,1). 5) DY/Dx designates how much the independent variable being true changes the outcome probability over that of the independent variable being false. 6) Bold estimates significant at p < 0.10.

Table A18: Probit Parameter Estimates for Likelihood of Favoring Increasing the Age of Eligibility from 65 to 67 in the Year 2000 to Address Medicare's Issues, n = 1,358

	Full Information Index Log Likelihood = -864.49			Benefits Information Index Log Likelihood = -858.23		
	Parameter Estimate	Parameter Est. for Interaction: Know*X_i	DY/Dx for Interaction	Parameter Estimate	Parameter Est. for Interaction: Know*X_i	DY/Dx for Interaction
Intercept	-0.33 (0.16)	--	--	-0.26 (0.20)	--	--
Less Well-Informed (ref)						
Well-informed	-0.01 (0.26)	--	--	-0.24 (0.26)	--	--
Age 18-49 (ref)						
Age 50-64	0.09 (0.17)	0.10 (0.27)	0.04	0.14 (0.19)	0.02 (0.26)	0.00
Age 65+	**0.50** (0.13)	0.12 (0.19)	0.05	**0.74** (0.18)	-0.17 (0.21)6	-0.06
Republican Party (ref)						
Democrat	**-0.29** (0.14)	0.26 (0.23)	0.10	-0.27 (0.18)	0.19 (0.22)	0.07
Independent/Other	-0.08 (0.13)	0.19 (0.22)	0.07	-0.06 (0.16)	0.18 (0.21)	0.07
Conservative ideology (ref)						
Moderate	-0.13 (0.12)	-0.07 (0.20)	-0.02	-0.21 (0.15)	0.07 (0.20)	0.03
Liberal	-0.10 (0.16)	-0.33 (0.27)	-0.12	-0.04 (0.20)	-0.38 (0.26)	-0.14
White race (ref)						
African-American	-0.13 (0.18)	-0.45 (0.39)	-0.16	-0.02 (0.22)	-0.60 (0.30)	**-0.21**
Asian/other	-0.20 (0.24)	-0.28 (0.43)	-0.10	-0.20 (0.26)	-0.25 (0.39)	0.09
Income < = $25,000 (ref)						
Income $25,001-$50,000	0.00 (0.13)	-0.02 (0.21)	-0.01	-0.02 (0.16)	0.08 (0.20)	0.03
Income >=$50,001	0.07 (0.15)	0.09 (0.25)	0.04	0.06 (0.18)	0.16 (0.24)	0.06
H.S. deg./equiv. or less (ref)						
some college	**0.31** (0.13)	0.16 (0.21)	0.06	**0.33** (0.16)	0.12 (0.21)	0.05
College/post. graduate deg.	**0.50** (0.14)	-0.16 (0.22)	-0.06	0.23 (0.16)	-0.37 (0.21)	*0.15*
Female (ref)						
Male	-0.08 (0.11)	0.09 (0.18)	0.04	0.04 (0.14)	-0.14 (0.18)	-0.05
Model χ^2	84.9			102		

Notes: 1) Model calculated using robust standard errors. 2) Standard errors of parameter estimates are in parantheses. 3) Model χ^2 tests for the overall fit of the model. 4) The interaction term is the knowledge Index (coded 0,1) multiplied by each independent variable (coded 0,1). 5) DY/Dx designates how much the independent variable being true changes the outcome probability over that of the independent variable being false. 6) Bold estimates significant at p < 0.10.

Table A19: Probit Parameter Estimates for Favoring a Reduction in Benefits to Medicare Recipients to Address Medicare's Issues, n = 1,343

	Full Information Index Log Likelihood = -606.10			Benefits Information Index Log Likelihood = -604.13		
	Parameter Estimate	Parameter Est. for Interaction: Know*X_i	DY/Dx for Interaction	Parameter Estimate	Parameter Est. for Interaction: Know*X_i	DY/Dx for Interaction
Intercept	**-0.67** (0.18)	--	--	**-0.88** (0.22)	--	--
Less Well-Informed (ref) Well-informed	**-0.79** (0.29)	--	--	-0.12 (0.30)	--	--
Age 18-49 (ref) Age 50-64	**-0.45** (0.22)	0.48 (0.32)	0.14	-0.34 (0.23)	0.15 (0.31)	0.04
Age 65+	**-0.28** (0.14)	**0.58** (0.22)	**0.18**	0.03 (0.19)	-0.08 (0.24)	-0.02
Republican Party (ref) Democrat	*-0.28* (0.16)	0.12 (0.26)	-0.03	-0.25 (0.20)	-0.10 (0.26)	-0.02
Independent/Other	*-0.25* (0.15)	0.21 (0.25)	0.06	-0.28 (0.18)	0.24 (0.24)	0.07
Conservative ideology (ref) Moderate	-0.19 (0.14)	-0.04 (0.22)	-0.01	-0.15 (0.17)	-0.14 (0.22)	-0.03
Liberal	-0.25 (0.19)	0.00 (0.33)	0.00	-0.13 (0.22)	-0.26 (0.31)	-0.06
White race (ref) African-American	*0.33* (0.18)	0.28 (0.38)	0.08	**0.59** (0.22)	*-0.60* (0.35)	*-0.12*
Asian/other	0.10 (0.25)	-0.13 (0.44)	-0.03	0.14 (0.27)	-0.18 (0.42)	-0.04
Income < = $25,000 (ref) Income $25,001-$50,000	0.21 (0.15)	-0.04 (0.25)	-0.01	*0.31* (0.19)	-0.26 (0.25)	-0.06
Income >=$50,001	0.15 (0.18)	0.10 (0.28)	0.02	*0.36* (0.21)	-0.34 (0.28)	-0.08
H.S. deg./equiv. or less (ref) some college	**-0.36** (0.16)	**0.63** (0.25)	**0.20**	**-0.41** (0.19)	**0.51** (0.25)	**0.15**
College/post. graduate deg.	0.00 (0.15)	*0.42* (0.24)	*0.12*	0.08 (0.15)	*0.45* (0.24)	*0.13*
Female (ref) Male	*0.22* (0.12)	**0.29** (0.20)	**0.08**	**0.33** (0.15)	0.02 (0.20)	0.00
Model χ^2	77.5			70.3		

Notes: 1) Model calculated using robust standard errors. 2) Standard errors of parameter estimates are in parantheses. 3) Model χ^2 tests for the overall fit of the model. 4) The interaction term is the knowledge Index (coded 0,1) multiplied by each independent variable (coded 0,1). 5) DY/Dx designates how much the independent variable being true changes the outcome probability over that of the independent variable being false. 6) Bold estimates significant at p < 0.10.

Table A20: Probit Parameter Estimates for Likelihood of Favoring an Increase in Premiums to Address Medicare's Issues, n = 1,337

	Full Information Index Log Likelihood = -812.64			Benefits Information Index Log Likelihood = -811.54		
	Parameter Estimate	Parameter Est. for Interaction: Know*X_i	DY/Dx for Interaction	Parameter Estimate	Parameter Est. for Interaction: Know*X_i	DY/Dx for Interaction
Intercept	-0.45 (0.16)	--	--	-0.32 (0.20)	--	--
Less Well-Informed (ref) Well-informed	-0.18 (0.27)	--	--	-0.39 (0.26)	--	--
Age 18-49 (ref) Age 50-64	0.03 (0.18)	-0.17 (0.28)	-0.06	-0.01 (0.20)	-0.04 (0.28)	-0.01
Age 65+	0.18 (0.13)	0.36 (0.20)	0.14	0.23 (0.17)	0.24 (0.21)	0.09
Republican Party (ref) Democrat	-0.14 (0.14)	-0.22 (0.22)	-0.08	-0.26 (0.17)	0.08 (0.22)	0.03
Independent/Other	-0.04 (0.13)	-0.39 (0.21)	-0.13	-0.26 (0.16)	0.20 (0.21)	0.07
Conservative ideology (ref) Moderate	0.03 (0.12)	0.04 (0.20)	0.01	-0.00 (0.15)	0.05 (0.19)	0.02
Liberal	-0.09 (0.16)	-0.02 (0.28)	-0.01	0.03 (0.20)	-0.25 (0.27)	-0.09
White race (ref) African-American	-0.11 (0.18)	-0.16 (0.40)	-0.05	-0.01 (0.22)	-0.34 (0.33)	-0.11
Asian/other	0.15 (0.24)	-0.11 (0.46)	-0.04	-0.01 (0.25)	0.34 (0.41)	0.13
Income < = $25,000 (ref) Income $25,001-$50,000	-0.02 (0.13)	-0.12 (0.22)	-0.04	0.00 (0.16)	-0.13 (0.21)	-0.05
Income >=$50,001	0.16 (0.16)	-0.03 (0.25)	-0.01	0.18 (0.18)	-0.01 (0.25)	-0.00
H.S. deg./equiv. or less (ref) some college	0.09 (0.13)	-0.06 (0.21)	-0.02	0.13 (0.16)	-0.09 (0.21)	-0.03 0.07
College/post. graduate deg.	0.40 (0.14)	0.00 (0.21)	0.00	0.30 (0.16)	0.20 (0.21)	
Female (ref) Male	-0.04 (0.11)	0.32 (0.18)	0.12	-0.02 (0.14)	0.15 (0.18)	0.06
Model χ^2	65.7			58.15		

Notes: 1) Model calculated using robust standard errors. 2) Standard errors of parameter estimates are in parantheses. 3) Model χ^2 tests for the overall fit of the model. 4) The interaction term is the knowledge Index (coded 0,1) multiplied by each independent variable (coded 0,1). 5) DY/Dx designates how much the independent variable being true changes the outcome probability over that of the independent variable being false. 6) Bold estimates significant at p < 0.10.

Appendix for Chapter Three

Table B1: Questions in 1988, 1992, and 1996 Used to Capture each Variable

Variable	Question and Coding
Vote	In talking to people about elections, we often find that a lot of people were not able to vote because they weren't registered, they were sick, or they just didn't have time. How about you-did you vote in the elections this November? coded: 1 if yes, 0 if no
Persuade	During the campaign, did you talk to any people and try to show them why they should vote for or against one of the parties or candidates? coded: 1 if yes, 0 if no
Age	What is the month, day and year of your birth? coded as dummy variables: Young Age 18-49 years (reference), Near-Old Age 50-64 years, Old Age (65+ years), and Near/Old Age 50-64

Income

Please look at this page and tell me the letter of the income group that includes the combined income of all members of your family living here in [year] before taxes. This figure should include salaries, wages, pensions, dividends, interest, and all other income. coded: 0 if 0-16th percentile, 0.25 if 17th-33rd percentile, 0.50 if 34th-67th percentile, 0.75 if 68th-95th percentile, 1 of 96th-100th percentile

1988	1992	1996
$0-$8,999	$0-$10,999	$0-11,999
$9,000-$16,999	$11,000-$19,999	$12,000-$24,999
$17,000-$34,999	$20,000-$44,999	$25,000-$49,999
$35,000-$74,999	$45,000-$104,999	$50,000-$104,999
$75,000+	$105,000+	$105,000+

Partner
employment

(If respondent is married or partnered) Is your husband/wife/partner working now, temporarily laid off, or unemployed, retired, permanently disabled, a homemaker, a student, or what? coded: 1 if partner is employed, 0 if otherwise

Education

What is the highest grade of school or year of college you have completed? Did you get a high school diploma or pass a high school equivalency test? What is the highest degree you have earned? coded as dummy variables: high school degree/equiv. (reference), no high school degree, some college/college degree

Table B2: Questions in 1988, 1992, and 1996 Used to Capture each Variable

Variable	Question and Coding
Religious service attendance	(1988) Do you go to a (church/synagogue)? (1992, 1996) Lots of things come up that keep people from attending religious services even if they want to. Thinking about you life these days, do you ever attend religious services, apart from occasional wedding, baptisms or funerals? coded: 1 if yes, 0 if no
Employed	We'd like to know if you are working now, temporarily laid off, or are unemployed, retired, permanently disabled, a homemaker, a student, or what? coded: 1 if employed, 0 otherwise
Union	Do you or does anyone else in this household belong to a labor union? coded: 1 if yes, 0 if no
Care which party wins	Generally, speaking, would you say that you personally care a good deal which party wins the presidential election this fall, or don't you care very much which party wins? coded: 1 if care a good deal, 0 if don't care very much
Attention to campaign on TV news	How much attention did you pay to news on TV about the campaign for president? coded as dummy variables: some (reference), none/very little, quite a bit/a great deal
Listen to campaign speech or discussion on radio	Did you listen to any speeches or discussions about the campaign on the radio? coded: 1 if yes, 0 if no

Internal
Efficacy

Now I'd like to read some of the kinds of things people tell us when we interview them. Please tell me whether you agree or disagree with these statements. Sometimes in politics and government seem so complicated that a person like me can't really understand what's going on. coded as dummy variables: low efficacy (reference), neutral, high efficacy

External
Efficacy

I don't think public officials care much what people like me think. People like me don't have much say about what government does. coded as dummy variables: low efficacy (reference), neutral, high efficacy

Table B3: Questions in 1988, 1992, and 1996 Used to Capture each Variable

Variable	Question and Coding
Political knowledge	Do you happen to know which party had the most members in the House of Representatives in Washington before the election (this/last) month? Do you happen to know which party had the most members in the U.S. Senate before the election (this/last) month? coded as dummy variables: none correct (reference), one correct, both correct
Perceived political knowledge	Respondent's general level of information about politics and public affairs seemed... coded as dummy variables: average (reference), low level, high level
Partisanship	Generally speaking, do you usually think of yourself as a Republican, Democrat, or what? (If Republican or Democrat) Would you call yourself a strong Republican/Democrat or not very strong Republican/Democrat? (If Independent, other, no preference) Do you think of yourself as closer to the Republican or Democratic party? coded as dummy variables: strong (reference), weak, independent leaning/independent
Contacted by political party	The political parties try to talk to as many people as they can to get them to vote for their candidate. Did anyone from one of the political parties call you up or come around to talk to you about the campaign this year? coded: 1 if contacted, 0 if not contacted

Community
ties   How long have you lived here in your
                            present (city/town/township/county)? coded:
                            actual number of years

Homeowner   (Do you/Does your family) own your
                            home, pay rent, or what? coded: 1 of owned, 0 if
                            not owned

African
American   coded: 1 if African American, 0 if not African
                  American

Sex   coded: 1 if female, 0 if male

Table B4: Descriptive statistics for respondents interviewed pre- and post-election

Variable	1988 % Yes or as indicated # of obs.	1992 % Yes or as indicated # of obs.	1996 % Yes or as indicated # of obs.
Vote	70 1770	76 2254	72 1534
Persuade	30 1771	39 2252	27 1533
Age			
18-49	64	67	63
50-64	21	17	19
65+	16 1772	16 2255	17 1534
Income			
0-16th percentiles	12	11	10
17-33rd percentiles	18	15	13
34-67th percentiles	32	28	28
68-95th percentiles	32	36	35
96th + percentiles	6 1636	10 2085	13 1404
Employed Spouse	43 1772	44 2255	42 1534
Education			
8 grades or less	9	6	5
9-11 grades, no deg.	12	11	12
HS diploma, equiv.	36	34	32
Some college	17	17	19
College deg.	26 1742	30 2198	32 1531
Attended religeous service attendance	86 1614	67 2250	71 1529
Epmloyed	67 1772	65 2244	66 1534
Union membership	22 1763	17 2244	19 1529

Table B5: Descriptive statistics for respondents interviewed pre- and post-election

Variable	1988 % Yes or as indicated # of obs.	1992 % Yes or as indicated # of obs.	1996 % Yes or as indicated # of obs.
Care which party wins	63 1742	77 2222	78 1532
Attention to campaign in TV news			
none	16	14	23
very little	13	10	14
some	29	28	28
quite a bit	27	29	22
a great deal	15 1772	20 2105	12 1534
Listen to campaign on radio	31 1772	36 2101	38 1528
Internal Efficacy			
Agree (low efficacy)	70	65	63
neutral	8	7	10
disagree	21 1758	28 2237	27 1528
External Efficacy			
Agree (low efficacy)	39	35	50
neutral	24	26	25
disagree	37 1747	39 2223	27 1525
Political knowledge			
both correct	49	46	62
one correct	16	19	16
none correct	35 1771	35 2255	22 1534

Table B6: Descriptive statistics for respondents interviewed pre- and post-election

Variable	1988 % Yes or as indicated # of obs.	1992 % Yes or as indicated # of obs.	1996 % Yes or as indicated # of obs.
Percieved Political knowledge			
very high	11	15	12
fairly high	28	31	26
average	32	35	37
fairly low	20	14	20
very low	8	5	6
	1764	2254	1497
Partisanship			
strong	32	29	31
weak	32	33	35
ind./learning	25	27	25
independent	10	11	9
	1747	2221	1518
Contacted by political party	24	21	27
	1771	2250	1532
Community ties	32.2	35.6	28.6
(average number of years)	1770	2248	1532
Homeowner	69	69	69
	1756	2116	1533
African American	12	13	12
	1768	2227	1527
Woman	55	53	55
	1772	2255	1534

Key to the following tables:

Variable	Definition	Reference category
ageold	Age 65+	Age <=64
nhigh	No high school degree	High School deg/equiv.
coll	Some college/college deg.	High School deg/equiv.
employ	Employed	Not employed
union	Union member in household	No union member
religion	Attend religious services	Has not attended services
income	Coded into five percentiles	
emplos	Employed spouse	Spouse not employed
commun	Number of years in community	
homeown	Own home	Does not own home
race	African American	Not African American
gender	Female	Male
care	Cares who wins election	Does not care
notv	None/very little attention to news about campaign on TV	Some attention
tv	Quite a bit/great deal of attention to campaign on TV	Some attention
listen	Listened to speeches, etc. on the radio	Did not listen to campaign on the radio
hknow	High perceived knowledge	Average perceived knowledge
lknow	Low perceived knowledge	Average perceived knowledge
weak	Weak partisanship	Strong partisanship
ind	Independent	Strong partisanship
nintff	Neutral internal efficacy	Low internal efficacy
hintff	High internal efficacy	Low internal efficacy
nextff	Neutral external efficacy	Low external efficacy
hextff	High external efficacy	Low external efficacy

Continued on next page

Variable	Definition	Reference category
bknow	Two of two knowledge questions correct	No correct knowledge questions
oknow	One of two knowledge questions correct	No correct knowl knowledge questions
mobile1	Contacted by a political party	Not contacted by a political party

Table B7: Survey Logistic Regression for Reporting of Vote in
1988 (Age 65+)

pweight: wgt			Number of obs		=	1435
Strata: strata			Number of strata		=	4
PSU: psu			Number of PSUs		=	47
			Population size		=	2625
			F(27, 17)		=	8.23
			Prob > F		=	0.0000

vote	Coef.	Std. Err.	t	P>|t|	[95% Conf. Interval]	
ageold	.4639744	.282269	1.644	0.108	-.1052752	1.033224
nhigh	-.2358369	.1900432	-1.241	0.221	-.6190955	.1474216
coll	.720439	.1986531	3.627	0.001	.3198168	1.121061
employ	-.0637412	.1721228	-0.370	0.713	-.4108599	.2833774
union	.3118823	.2133109	1.462	0.151	-.1183002	.7420648
religion	.7118216	.2092982	3.401	0.001	.2897316	1.133912
income	1.127369	.4257214	2.648	0.011	.2688197	1.985917
emplos	.0909609	.2066666	0.440	0.662	-.325822	.5077438
commun	.007528	.0026359	2.856	0.007	.0022121	.0128439
homeown	.4028111	.1930704	2.086	0.043	.0134476	.7921747
race	-.1112176	.284898	-0.390	0.698	-.6857691	.4633339
gender	.1913748	.1686694	1.135	0.263	-.1487795	.5315292
care	.6141884	.1937128	3.171	0.003	.2235293	1.004847
notv	-.1608039	.1573656	-1.022	0.313	-.4781619	.1565541
tv	.1625264	.1749629	0.929	0.358	-.19032	.5153728
listen	.2268283	.1944442	1.167	0.250	-.1653057	.6189623
hknow	.5817254	.1902636	3.057	0.004	.1980222	.9654285
lknow	-.3358422	.2176458	-1.543	0.130	-.7747668	.1030823
weak	-.6495787	.1682739	-3.860	0.000	-.9889354	-.310222
ind	-1.173924	.2018193	-5.817	0.000	-1.580931	.7669162
nintff	-.0344899	.2390828	-0.144	0.886	-.5166463	.4476665
hintff	561312	.2174357	2.582	0.013	.122811	.999813
nextff	.522198	.1986333	2.629	0.012	.1216158	.9227802
hextff	.1795857	.2100253	0.855	0.397	-.2439707	.6031421
bknow	.6530101	.1933299	3.378	0.002	.2631232	1.042897
oknow	.238883	.2200368	1.086	0.284	-.2048634	.6826295
mobile1	.9599613	.1819976	5.275	0.000	.5929282	1.326994
_cons	-1.732977	.481324	-3.600	0.001	-2.703659	.7622949

Table B8: Survey Logistic Regression for Reporting of Vote in 1992 (Age 65+)

pweight: wgt			Number of obs	=	1876	
Strata: strata			Number of strata	=	4	
PSU: psu			Number of PSUs	=	65	
			Population size	=	1884.597	
			F(27, 35)	=	19.39	
			Prob > F	=	0.0000	

vote	Coef.	Std. Err.	t	P>|t|	[95% Conf. Interval]	
ageold	.5967637	.2155315	2.769	0.007	.1657819	1.027746
nhigh	-1.0295	.1965002	-5.239	0.000	-1.422427	-.636574
coll	.6182322	.1965161	3.146	0.003	.225274	1.01119
employ	.2510935	.1714962	1.464	0.148	-.0918344	.5940214
union	.7021903	.2393416	2.934	0.005	.2235972	1.180784
religion	.265614	.1443389	1.840	0.071	-.0230094	.5542374
income	.3932344	.2777016	1.416	0.162	-.1620643	.9485332
emplos	.1401045	.1573994	0.890	0.377	-.1746351	.4548441
commun	.0019833	.0021001	0.944	0.349	-.0022161	.0061828
homeown	.6356635	.137007	4.640	0.000	.3617011	.9096259
race	.2890361	.2363898	1.223	0.226	-.1836545	.7617267
gender	.5940176	.1564857	3.796	0.000	.2811051	.9069301
care	.7308698	.1520925	4.805	0.000	.426742	1.034998
notv	-.3166065	.1534505	-2.063	0.043	-.6234497	-.0097633
tv	.4846294	.157113	3.085	0.003	.1704626	.7987961
listen	.2630795	.1749162	1.504	0.138	-.0866871	.6128461
hknow	.3575742	.1612495	2.218	0.030	.0351361	.6800124
lknow	-.3705824	.1736562	-2.134	0.037	-.7178293	-.0233355
weak	-.5776351	.1776024	-3.252	0.002	-.9327731	-.2224971
ind	-.777155	.1531248	-5.075	0.000	-1.083347	-.470963
nintff	-.5116639	.2494805	-2.051	0.045	-1.010531	-.0127968
hintff	.1286193	.1734	0.742	0.461	-.2181155	.4753541
nextff	.1608179	.1845966	0.871	0.387	-.2083057	.5299415
hextff	.0908392	.1673	0.543	0.589	-.2436977	.4253762
bknow	.8452934	.1771095	4.773	0.000	.491141	1.199446
oknow	.4721461	.1815546	2.601	0.012	.1091053	.8351869
mobile1	.9514069	.2154061	4.417	0.000	.5206758	1.382138
_cons	-1.257712	.3088417	-4.072	0.000	-1.875279	-.6401445

Table B9: Survey Logistic Regression for Reporting a Vote in 1996
(Age 65+)

pweight: wgt   Number of obs   =   1372
Strata: strata   Number of strata =   4
PSU: psu   Number of PSUs   =   115
                        Population size =1373.2362
                        F(27,   85)   =   9.34
                        Prob > F   =   0.0000

vote	Coef.	Std. Err.	t	P>|t|	[95% Conf. Interval]	
ageold	.8174809	.3091993	2.644	0.009	.2047818	1.43018
nhigh	-.7320476	.2839312	-2.578	0.011	-1.294676	-.1694191
coll	.3920661	.2291498	1.711	0.090	-.0620095	.8461417
employ	-.1693959	.2317733	-0.731	0.466	-.6286702	.2898783
union	.4444821	.239339	1.857	0.066	-.029784	.9187482
religion	.7179273	.2125378	3.378	0.001	.2967695	1.139085
income |1	.7896924	.3872563	2.039	0.044	.0223183	1.557067
emplos	.3492352	.1956017	1.785	0.077	-.0383627	.7368331
commun	-.0046573	.003786	-1.230	0.221	-.0121596	.002845
homeown	.3681821	.1708413	2.155	0.033	.0296487	.7067156
race	-.0992256	.2780098	-0.357	0.722	-.6501205	.4516693
gender	.2555175	.2136918	1.196	0.234	-.1679269	.678962
care	.5723018	213703	2.678	0.009	.1488351	.9957685
notv	-.0574887	234486	-0.245	0.807	-.5221383	.4071609
tv	.7540594	.2461529	3.063	0.003	.2662911	1.241828
listen	.4159235	.2062548	2.017	0.046	.0072158	.8246311
hknow	.4177377	.2581291	1.618	0.108	-.0937622	.9292377
lknow	-.4685051	.1881998	-2.489	0.014	-.8414356	-.0955746
weak	-1.11833	.2264733	-4.938	0.000	-1.567102	-.6695579
ind	-1.206547	.2413379	-4.999	0.000	-1.684774	-.7283199
nintff	.1688385	.344031	0.491	0.625	-.5128818	.8505589
hintff	-.1274141	.1982065	-0.643	0.522	-.5201735	.2653454
nextff	.4112326	.2381044	1.727	0.087	-.0605872	.8830524
hextff	.3047596	.2070828	1.472	0.144	-.1055888	.7151081
bknow	.5567257	.2098405	2.653	0.009	.1409128	.9725386
oknow	.1902374	.2512527	0.757	0.451	-.3076367	.6881115
mobile1	.7424845	.2412878	3.077	0.003	.2643566	1.220612
_cons	-.8303986	.3736631	-2.222	0.028	-1.570837	.0899604

Table B10: Survey Logistic Regression for Reporting a Vote in 1988 (Democrats Age 65+)

```
pweight: wgt              Number of obs    =   518
Strata:  strata          Number of strata  =    4
PSU:     psu             Number of PSUs    =   47
                         Population size   =   952
                         F( 27,    85)     =  4.94
                         Prob > F          = 0.0005
```

vote	Coef.	Std. Err.	t	P>|t|	[95% Conf. Interval]	
ageold	-.0974799	.436304	-0.223	0.824	-.9773709	.7824111
nhigh	-.0341484	.2666399	-0.128	0.899	-.5718791	.5035823
coll	.638584	.3011363	2.121	0.040	.0312847	1.245883
employ	.0243704	.2843021	0.086	0.932	-.5489793	.5977201
union	.6794671	.3550582	1.914	0.062	-.036576	1.39551
religion	.8734443	.3317045	2.633	0.012	.2044983	1.54239
income	.4665162	.6877529	0.678	0.501	-.9204697	1.853502
emplos	.5384137	.2861384	1.882	0.067	-.0386393	1.115467
commun	.0068764	.0046979	1.464	0.151	-.0025979	.0163507
homeown	-.0483341	.2662754	-0.182	0.857	-.5853296	.4886614
race	.1793199	.3443568	0.521	0.605	-.5151417	.8737815
gender	.329338	.2880237	1.143	0.259	-.2515171	.9101932
care	.3315756	.282667	1.173	0.247	-.2384766	.9016278
notv	-.2135175	.2383311	-0.896	0.375	-.6941579	.2671229
tv	-.1149935	.255781	-0.450	0.655	-.6308251	.400838
listen	.6160728	.281135	2.191	0.034	.0491101	1.183035
hknow	.2947201	.3581698	0.823	0.415	-.4275982	1.017038
lknow	-.1643445	.2911035	-0.565	0.575	-.7514106	.4227216
weak	-.6890842	.257074	-2.680	0.010	-1.207525	-.1706432
nintff	-.2089345	.4603122	-0.454	0.652	-1.137243	.7193736
hintff	-.1062063	.3386528	-0.314	0.755	-.7891647	.5767521
nextff	1.042938	.3713289	2.809	0.007	.2940818	1.791794
hextff	.4373346	.2967176	1.474	0.148	-.1610534	1.035723
bknow	.711929	.3210784	2.217	0.032	.0644127	1.359445
oknow	.2860436	.3997216	0.716	0.478	-.5200719	1.092159
mobile1	1.127107	.313018	3.601	0.001	.4958458	1.758368
_cons	-1.790149	.7375198	-2.427	0.019	-3.2775	-.3027989

Table B11: Survey Logistic Regression for Reporting a Vote in 1992 (Democrats Age 65+)

pweight:	wgt	Number of obs	=	660	
Strata:	strata	Number of strata	=	4	
PSU:	psu	Number of PSUs	=	65	
		Population size	=	662.8329	
		F(27, 85)	=	3.88	
		Prob > F	=	0.0001	

vote	Coef.	Std. Err.	t	P>|t|	[95% Conf. Interval]	
ageold	.6656735	.3883483	1.714	0.092	-.1108767	1.442224
nhigh	-.9019111	.2783233	-3.241	0.002	-1.458453	-.3453693
coll	.4582795	.3371665	1.359	0.179	-.2159266	1.132486
employ	.648727	.3037881	2.135	0.037	.0412652	1.256189
union	.6378905	.4394684	1.452	0.152	-.2408809	1.516662
religion	-.2182488	.3097335	-0.705	0.484	-.8375992	.4011015
income	.3044645	.6947947	0.438	0.663	-1.084863	1.693792
emplos	.3376152	.300377	1.124	0.265	-.2630257	.9382562
commun	.0104342	.0035874	2.909	0.005	.0032606	.0176077
homeown	.6544355	.2944869	2.222	0.030	.0655726	1.243298
race	.2636922	.3014747	0.875	0.385	-.3391437	.8665281
gender	.705377	.2557325	2.758	0.008	.1940083	1.216746
care	.3334823	.3200226	1.042	0.301	-.3064423	.973407
notv	-.3728777	.3390125	-1.100	0.276	-1.050775	.3050197
tv	.6833354	.3027904	2.257	0.028	.0778686	1.288802
listen	.0427422	.2533334	0.169	0.867	-.4638293	.5493137
hknow	.8348557	.3261969	2.559	0.013	.1825846	1.487127
lknow	-.1206492	.3394621	-0.355	0.724	-.7994454	.5581471
weak	-.7416808	.2777739	-2.670	0.010	-1.297124	-.1862376
nintff	-.1486269	.5291567	-0.281	0.780	-1.206741	.9094872
hintff	.5278393	.3143978	1.679	0.098	-.1008379	1.156517
nextff	.3417115	.3363691	1.016	0.314	-.3309001	1.014323
hextff	-.0195202	.2910857	-0.067	0.947	-.601582	.5625417
bknow	.7385491	328258	2.250	0.028	.0821568	1.394941
oknow	.6042484	.3898829	1.550	0.126	-.1753706	1.383867
mobile1	.8933982	.4075681	2.192	0.032	.0784156	1.708381
_cons	-1.481357	.5415981	-2.735	0.00	-2.564349	-.3983645

Table B12: Survey Logistic Regression for Reporting a Vote in 1996 (Democrats Age 65+)

pweight:	wgt		Number of obs	=	543
Strata:	strata		Number of strata	=	4
PSU:	psu		Number of PSUs	=	97
			Population size	=	532.8329
			F(26, 68)	=	4.17
			Prob > F	=	0.0000

vote	Coef.	Std. Err	t	P>|t|	[95% Conf. Interval]	
ageold	.7740083	.4782193	1.619	0.109	-.1756404	1.723657
nhigh	-.4082999	.3461285	-1.180	0.241	-1.095642	.2790426
coll	.6506	.4112777	1.582	0.117	-.166116	1.467316
employ	.1253718	.3514514	0.357	0.722	-.5725409	.8232846
union	.8425429	.4059303	2.076	0.041	.0364457	1.64864
religion	.872541	.292224	2.986	0.004	.292242	1.45284
income	.6214792	.7135657	0.871	0.386	-.7955207	2.038479
emplos	.8017867	.349966	2.291	0.024	.1068236	1.49675
commun	-.0051499	.0053757	-0.958	0.341	-.0158249	.0055251
homeown	.4763213	.333584	1.428	0.157	-.1861103	1.138753
race	-.1274241	.3764741	-0.338	0.736	-.875027	.6201788
gender	.0438968	.3216437	0.136	0.892	-.5948239	.6826176
care	.4925008	.3673071	1.341	0.183	-.2368983	1.2219
notv	-.5390954	.3787681	-1.423	0.158	-1.291254	.213063
tv	.4791204	.3879103	1.235	0.220	-.2911925	1.249433
listen	.3150936	.3788028	0.832	0.408	-.4371336	1.067321
hknow	.7566603	.3709053	2.040	0.044	.0201158	1.493205
lknow	-.0297486	3565165	-0.083	0.934	-.7377197	.6782224
weak	-1.156255	.3429383	-3.372	0.001	-1.837263	-.4752476
nintff	.1209421	.5368173	0.225	0.822	-.9450707	1.186955
hintff	.1748617	.3584388	0.488	0.627	-.5369268	.8866502
nextff	.6874174	.3850965	1.785	0.078	-.0773079	1.452143
hextff	.1236894	.3283867	0.377	0.707	-.5284215	.7758003
bknow	.2153909	.3442165	0.626	0.533	-.4681548	.8989365
oknow	-.4629734	.4673239	-0.991	0.324	-1.390986	.4650392
mobile1	1.094198	.4499487	2.432	0.017	.2006887	1.987706
_cons	-.9851489	.738141	-1.335	0.185	-2.450951	.4806528

Table B13: Survey Logistic Regression for Reporting a Vote in 1988 (Independents Age 65+)

pweight: wgt			Number of obs	=	434
Strata: strata			Number of strata	=	4
PSU: psu			Number of PSUs	=	47
			Population size	=	811
			F(25, 19)	=	5.34
			Prob > F	=	0.0002

vote	Coef.	Std. Err.	t	P>|t|	[95% Conf. Interval]	
ageold	.8116242	.4233206	1.917	0.062	-.042083	1.665331
nhigh	-.8572045	.3456213	-2.480	0.017	-1.554216	-.1601927
coll	.7301364	.3643905	2.004	0.051	-.0047271	1.465
employ	-.2866257	.3520024	-0.814	0.420	-.9965062	.4232549
union	.2182616	.328356	0.665	0.510	-.4439313	.8804545
religion	.539549	.4028641	1.339	0.188	-.2729039	1.352002
income	1.460785	.7116556	2.053	0.046	.0255945	2.895975
emplos	-.1667499	.3715036	-0.449	0.656	-.9159583	.5824586
commun	.0109189	.0046303	2.358	0.023	.0015809	.0202568
homeown	.5394476	.3779058	1.427	0.161	-.2226722	1.301567
race	-.3255772	.4611128	-0.706	0.484	-1.2555	.6043455
gender	.3917711	.3315705	1.182	0.244	-.2769044	1.060447
care	1.010532	.2920194	3.460	0.001	.4216187	1.599445
notv	-.0633326	.3710111	-0.171	0.865	-.8115479	.6848827
tv	.6221829	.3794107	1.640	0.108	-.1429716	1.387337
listen	.4391333	.4460082	0.985	0.330	-.4603279	1.338595
hknow	.5346752	.304415	1.756	0.086	-.0792362	1.148587
lknow	-.6965126	.3489032	-1.996	0.052	-1.400143	.0071178
nintff	-.0335222	.5225757	-0.064	0.949	-1.087396	1.020352
hintff	1.580636	.4906957	3.221	0.002	.5910534	2.570218
nextff	.0624308	.3975303	0.157	0.876	-.7392654	.864127
hextff	-.4087716	.4215306	-0.970	0.338	-1.258869	.4413259
bknow	.6877262	.3286126	2.093	0.042	.0250158	1.350437
oknow	.2902164	.3442882	0.843	0.404	-.4041069	.9845397
mobile1	.9614059	.4040297	2.380	0.022	.1466024	1.776209
_cons	-3.009908	.5992782	-5.023	0.000	-4.218468	-1.801348

Table B14: Survey Logistic Regression for Reporting a Vote in 1992 (Independents Age 65+)

pweight: wgt	Number of obs	=	631
Strata: strata	Number of strata	=	4
PSU: psu	Number of PSUs	=	64
	Population size	=	632.7741
	F(25, 36)	=	6.43
	Prob > F	=	0.0000

vote	Coef.	Std. Err.	t	P>|t|	[95% Conf. Interval]	
ageold	.9015656	.3581676	2.517	0.015	.1851237	1.618007
nhigh	-1.505871	.3829566	-3.932	0.000	-2.271898	-.7398439
coll	.6679521	.2649382	2.521	0.014	.1379969	1.197907
employ	.3493811	.2568008	1.361	0.179	-.1642969	.8630591
union	.6330367	.3335188	1.898	0.063	-.0341001	1.300174
religion	.4423263	.2531712	1.747	0.086	-.0640914	.948744
income	.7577136	.5917606	1.280	0.205	-.4259837	1.941411
emplos	.0539283	.2636375	0.205	0.839	-.4734251	.5812817
commun	.0040101	.0039627	1.012	0.316	-.0039164	.0119366
homeown	.4672243	.2420388	1.930	0.058	-.0169254	.9513739
race	.3124686	.4276525	0.731	0.468	-.5429637	1.167901
gender	.6535299	.3242136	2.016	0.048	.0050062	1.302054
care	.8464595	.2227497	3.800	0.000	.4008939	1.292025
notv	-.3223642	.2370004	-1.36	0.179	-.7964355	.1517071
tv	.255757	.3051687	0.838	0.405	-.3546713	.8661853
listen	.1747477	.3023146	0.578	0.565	-.4299715	.7794668
hknow	.0624702	.3076106	0.203	0.840	-.5528426	.6777829
lknow	-.6254713	.2813578	-2.223	0.030	-1.188271	-.0626719
nintff	-.5836231	.3680587	-1.586	0.118	-1.31985	.1526039
hintff	-.0048956	.303783	-0.016	0.987	-.612552	.6027608
nextff	.1140806	.2910381	0.392	0.696	-.4680823	.6962436
hextff	.2319131	.2862468	0.810	0.421	-.3406656	.8044919
bknow	1.207443	.2886533	4.183	0.000	.6300507	1.784836
oknow	.8230837	.2811416	2.928	0.005	.2607168	1.385451
mobile1	1.080978	.3147869	3.434	0.001	.4513109	1.710646
_cons	-2.276635	.5268525	-4.321	0.000	-3.330497	-1.222773

Table B15: Survey Logistic Regression for Reporting a Vote in 1996 (Independents Age 65+)

pweight: wgt   Number of obs = 353
Strata: strata   Number of strata = 4
PSU: psu   Number of PSUs = 85
Population size = 381.7859
$F(25, 36)$ = 6.43
Prob > F = 0.0023

vote	Coef.	Std. Err.	t	P>|t|	[95% Conf. Interval]	
ageold	1.478829	.6295039	2.349	0.021	.2263133	2.731344
nhigh	-1.018441	.5640072	-1.806	0.075	-2.140639	.1037563
coll	.3097777	.4056691	0.764	0.447	-.4973765	1.116932
employ	-.3540733	.4178889	-0.847	0.399	-1.185541	.4773945
union	-.0231982	.3529871	-0.066	0.948	-.7255317	.6791354
religion	.4276252	.3660613	1.168	0.246	-.3007219	1.155972
income	1.840213	.6605256	2.786	0.007	.5259747	3.154452
emplos	-.1822843	.3922792	-0.465	0.643	-.9627968	.5982283
commun	.0056969	.0068113	0.836	0.405	-.0078554	.0192493
homeown	.2209887	.3498736	0.632	0.529	-.47515	.9171275
race	-.3279478	.5597859	-0.586	0.560	-1.441746	.7858506
gender	.3456481	.4032184	0.857	0.394	-.45663	1.147926
care	.5784904	.4555405	1.270	0.208	-.3278923	1.484873
notv	.3622725	.3127302	1.158	0.250	-.2599624	.9845075
tv	1.138925	.4225509	2.695	0.009	.2981817	1.979669
listen	-.2199925	.3517412	-0.625	0.533	-.9198471	.4798621
hknow	.5361022	.3635478	1.475	0.144	-.1872439	1.259448
lknow	-1.080052	.3576231	-3.020	0.003	-1.79161	-.3684945
nintff	.7093549	.7056742	1.005	0.318	-.6947154	2.113425
hintff	-.3473178	.328478	-1.057	0.293	-1.000886	.3062504
nextff	.4673138	.349279	1.338	0.185	-.2276418	1.162269
hextff	.154372	.4584472	0.337	0.737	-.7577941	1.066538
bknow	.2233407	.4088781	0.546	0.586	-.5901985	1.03688
oknow	.3565477	.4618141	0.772	0.442	-.5623175	1.275413
mobile1	.2601813	.3370412	0.772	0.442	-.410425	.9307875
_cons	-1.777086	.6605034	-2.691	0.009	-3.091281	-.4628917

Table B16: Survey Logistic Regression for Attempting to Persuade Another's Vote in 1988 (Age 65+)

pweight: wgt			Number of obs	=	1436
Strata: strata			Number of strata	=	4
PSU: psu			Number of PSUs	=	47
			Population size	=	2626
			F(25, 36)	=	6.89
			Prob > F	=	0.0001

persuad	Coef.	Std. Err.	t	P>|t|	[95% Conf. Interval]	
ageold	-.481077	.2045964	-2.351	0.023	-.893685	-.0684691
nhigh	-.2177806	.2100168	-1.037	0.306	-.6413199	.2057587
coll	.1896671	.1634868	1.160	0.252	-.1400355	.5193697
employ	.0182192	.1627253	0.112	0.911	-.3099477	.346386
union	-.028332	.1708056	-0.166	0.869	-.3727944	.3161304
religion	.0881749	.1729267	0.510	0.613	-.2605651	.4369149
income	.1428101	.2801984	0.510	0.613	-.4222638	.707884
emplos	.1785774	.1218203	1.466	0.150	-.0670965	.4242514
commun	-.0019422	.0028062	-0.692	0.493	-.0076015	.0037171
homeown	.0214002	.1715193	0.125	0.901	-.3245015	.3673019
race	.0942419	.2958455	0.319	0.75	-.5023874	.6908712
gender	-.3510017	.1408046	-2.493	0.017	-.6349611	-.0670423
care	.5844384	.1539658	3.796	0.000	.2739368	.89494
notv	-.1500799	.1631777	-0.920	0.363	-.479159	.1789992
tv	.5186198	.1855046	2.796	0.008	.1445141	.8927255
listen	.1754044	.1488265	1.179	0.245	-.1247328	.4755416
hknow	.3708282	.1788422	2.073	0.044	.0101586	.7314978
lknow	.0366194	.2306317	0.159	0.875	-.4284938	.5017327
weak	-.4324898	.1610027	-2.686	0.010	-.7571827	-.1077968
ind	-.3886043	.1613895	-2.408	0.020	-.7140774	-.0631313
nintff	.479929	.2355618	2.037	0.048	.0048733	.9549846
hintff	.3043249	.1686762	1.804	0.078	-.0358431	.6444928
nextff	3303638	.1804791	1.830	0.074	-.033607	.6943347
hextff	.0792635	.1553255	0.510	0.612	-.2339802	.3925073
bknow	.3698815	.2354192	1.571	0.123	-.1048866	.8446497
oknow	.4537191	.2358454	1.924	0.061	-.0219084	.9293466
mobile1	.4128045	.1790454	2.306	0.026	.0517251	.773884
_cons	-1.985962	.409572	-4.849	0.000	-2.811943	-1.159981

Table B17: Survey Logistic Regression for Attempting to Persuade
Another's Vote in 1992 (Age 65+)

pweight:	wgt		Number of obs	=	1876
Strata:	strata		Number of strata	=	4
PSU:	psu		Number of PSUs	=	65
			Population size	=	1884.401
			F(27, 35)	=	7.77
			Prob > F	=	0.0000

persuad	Coef.	Std. Err.	t	P>|t|	[95% Conf. Interval]	
ageold	-.9828044	.1950669	-5.038	0.000	-1.372865	-.5927441
nhigh	-.1376199	.2117283	-0.650	0.518	-.5609969	.2857571
coll	.0718102	.1219355	0.589	0.558	-.1720149	.3156354
employ	.0077939	.1291794	0.060	0.952	-.2505162	.266104
union	-.1119122	.1573656	-0.711	0.480	-.4265841	.2027597
religion	.1007788	.1337551	0.753	0.454	-.1666811	.3682386
income	-.5021513	.3096922	-1.621	0.110	-1.121419	.1171164
emplos	.1127923	.1398635	0.806	0.423	-.1668821	.3924666
commun	-.0031237	.0016668	-1.874	0.066	-.0064567	.0002092
homeown	.0350382	.1461253	0.240	0.811	-.2571574	.3272339
race	-.5460354	.23306	-2.343	0.022	-1.012068	-.0800032
gender	-.3062397	.1348729	-2.271	0.027	-.5759348	-.0365446
care	.7194146	.1583016	4.545	0.000	.4028709	1.035958
notv	-.1541414	.1709471	-0.902	0.371	-.4959713	.1876885
tv	.3188142	.1380566	2.309	0.024	.0427529	.5948754
listen	.0421851	.1106003	0.381	0.704	-.1789739	.2633441
hknow	.1125574	.1345302	0.837	0.406	-.1564523	.3815672
lknow	-.7462344	.2034504	-3.668	0.001	-1.153059	-.3394101
weak	-.5652512	.1352969	-4.178	0.000	-.8357939	-.2947084
ind	-.513078	.1262344	-4.064	0.000	-.7654993	-.2606567
nintff	.0503631	.2175875	0.231	0.818	-.38473	.4854563
hintff	.1901227	.132467	1.435	0.156	-.0747615	.4550069
nextff	.2277962	.1625629	1.401	0.166	-.0972685	.5528608
hextff	.2033874	.1573252	1.293	0.201	-.1112037	.5179785
bknow	.3871422	.1428102	2.711	0.009	.1015757	.6727088
oknow	.6564238	.1652553	3.972	0.000	.3259754	.9868722
mobile1	.5984407	.1483912	4.033	0.000	.3017142	.8951672
_cons	-.7647723	.311516	-2.455	0.017	-1.387687	-.1418575

Table B18: Survey Logistic Regression for Attempting to Persuade Another's Vote in 1996 (Age 65+)

pweight:	wgt		Number of obs	=	1372
Strata:	strata		Number of strata	=	4
PSU:	psu		Number of PSUs	=	115
			Population size	=	1373.2362
			F(27, 85)	=	6.35
			Prob > F	=	0.0000

persuad	Coef.	Std. Err.	t	P>|t|	[95% Conf. Interval]	
ageold	-.2900132	.2486767	-1.166	0.246	-.7827827	.2027564
nhigh	-.0764772	.2857545	-0.268	0.789	-.6427189	.4897645
coll	-.2382905	.171235	-1.392	0.167	-.5776041	.101023
employ	-.1248736	.1707672	-0.731	0.466	-.4632601	.213513
union	.1404294	.1831872	0.767	0.445	-.2225683	.5034271
religion	.3230094	.1653924	1.953	0.053	-.0047266	.6507454
income	.0490158	.3672037	0.133	0.894	-.6786227	.7766543
emplos	.2266639	.1433869	1.581	0.117	-.0574668	.5107946
commun	-.0079477	.0024779	-3.207	0.002	-.0128578	-.0030376
homeown	.0468768	.1775962	0.264	0.792	-.305042	.3987956
race	-.0839793	.2536894	-0.331	0.741	-.5866816	-.4187231
gender	-.3461949	.1477443	-2.343	0.021	-.6389602	-.0534297
care	.5862916	.2574387	2.277	0.025	.0761597	1.096424
notv	.3578741	.1837511	1.948	0.054	-.006241	.7219892
tv	.6610909	.1697916	3.894	0.000	.3246376	.9975442
listen	.565859	.1526994	3.706	0.000	.2632749	.8684431
hknow	.4019703	.1602586	2.508	0.014	.0844071	.7195335
lknow	-.5471294	.2651403	-2.064	0.041	-1.072523	-.0217362
weak	-.5306695	.1743268	-3.044	0.003	-.8761097	-.1852293
ind	-.2290594	.1982632	-1.155	0.250	-.6219311	.1638123
nintff	.2544201	.2277801	1.117	0.266	-.1969414	.7057816
hintff	.0535986	.1899993	0.282	0.778	-.3228977	.4300949
nextff	.0239358	.2023456	0.118	0.906	-.3770255	.4248971
hextff	-.1145765	.1818722	-0.630	0.530	-.4749685	.2458155
bknow	.2342102	.2501719	0.936	0.351	-.2615221	.7299425
oknow	.3143305	.3098943	1.014	0.313	-.2997456	.9284067
mobile1	.4543058	.1372415	3.310	0.001	.1823527	.726259
_cons	-1.969528	.4305653	-4.574	0.000	-2.822722	-1.116334

Table B19: Survey Logistic Regression for Attempting to Persuade
Another's Vote in 1988 (Democrats Age 65+)

pweight:	wgt		Number of obs	=	1436
Strata:	strata		Number of strata	=	4
PSU:	psu		Number of PSUs	=	47
			Population size	=	2626
			F(27, 17)	=	6.89
			Prob > F	=	0.0001

persuad	Coef.	Std. Err.	t	P>|t|	[95% Conf. Interval]	
ageold	-.481077	.2045964	-2.351	0.023	-.893685	-.0684691
nhigh	-.2177806	.2100168	-1.037	0.306	-.6413199	.2057587
coll	.1896671	.1634868	1.160	0.252	-.1400355	.5193697
employ	.0182192	.1627253	0.112	0.911	-.3099477	.346386
union	-.028332	.1708056	-0.166	0.869	-.3727944	.3161304
religion	.0881749	.1729267	0.510	0.613	-.2605651	.4369149
income	.1428101	.2801984	0.510	0.613	-.4222638	.707884
emplos	.1785774	.1218203	1.466	0.150	-.0670965	.4242514
commun	-.0019422	.0028062	-0.692	0.493	-.0076015	.0037171
homeown	.0214002	.1715193	0.125	0.901	-.3245015	.3673019
race	.0942419	.2958455	0.319	0.752	-.5023874	.6908712
gender	-.3510017	.1408046	-2.493	0.017	-.6349611	-.0670423
care	.5844384	.1539658	3.796	0.000	.2739368	.89494
notv	-.1500799	.1631777	-0.920	0.363	-.479159	.1789992
tv	.5186198	.1855046	2.796	0.008	.1445141	.8927255
listen	.1754044	.1488265	1.179	0.245	-.1247328	.4755416
hknow	.3708282	.1788422	2.073	0.044	.0101586	.7314978
lknow	.0366194	.2306317	0.159	0.875	-.4284938	.5017327
weak	-.4324898	.1610027	-2.686	0.010	-.7571827	-.1077968
ind	-.3886043	.1613895	-2.408	0.020	-.7140774	-.0631313
nintff	.479929	.2355618	2.037	0.048	.0048733	.9549846
hintff	.3043249	.1686762	1.804	0.078	-.0358431	.6444928
nextff	.3303638	.1804791	1.830	0.074	-.033607	.6943347
hextff	.0792635	.1553255	0.510	0.612	-.2339802	.3925073
bknow	.3698815	.2354192	1.571	0.123	-.1048866	.8446497
oknow	.4537191	.2358454	1.924	0.061	-.0219084	.9293466
mobile1	.4128045	.1790454	2.306	0.026	.0517251	.773884
_cons	-1.985962	.409572	-4.849	0.000	-2.811943	-1.159981

Table B20: Survey Logistic Regression for Attempting to Persuade
Another's Vote in 1992 (Democrats Age 65+)

pweight:	wgt		Number of obs	=	660	
Strata:	strata		Number of strata	=	4	
PSU:	psu		Number of PSUs	=	65	
			Population size	=	662.8329	
			F(26, 36)	=	2.50	
			Prob > F	=	0.0056	

persuad	Coef.	Std. Err.	t	P>|t|	[95% Conf. Interval]	
ageold	-.592793	.3208738	-1.847	0.070	-1.23442	.0488338
nhigh	-.1635624	.3344911	-0.489	0.627	-.8324186	.5052938
coll	.428058	.2677602	1.599	0.115	-.1073617	.9634776
employ	-.1243757	.2235706	-0.556	0.580	-.5714328	.3226814
union	-.1138274	.2391633	-0.476	0.636	-.5920639	-.3644091
religion	.0143076	.2364748	0.061	0.952	-.458553	.4871682
income	-.8187237	.4793015	-1.708	0.093	-1.777146	.1396989
emplos	.3915012	.2438257	1.606	0.114	-.0960584	.8790608
commun	-.0029859	.0029052	-1.028	0.308	-.0087953	.0028235
homeown	.0520862	.1829301	0.285	0.777	-.3137052	.4178776
race	-.2900538	.2805034	-1.034	0.305	-.8509551	.2708475
gender	-.2826821	.1924728	-1.469	0.147	-.6675552	.1021909
care	1.179525	.3018348	3.908	0.000	.5759687	1.783081
notv	-.135779	.4080242	-0.333	0.740	-.9516738	.6801157
tv	.2209451	.2074033	1.065	0.291	-.1937834	.6356736
listen	.1790985	.1881833	0.952	0.345	-.1971972	.5553943
hknow	.1423415	.228865	0.622	0.536	-.3153023	.5999852
lknow	-.6272952	.4039302	-1.553	0.126	-1.435004	.1804131
weak	-.4092924	.1894805	-2.160	0.035	-.7881821	-.0304028
nintff	.111894	.3842168	0.291	0.772	-.6563949	.8801829
hintff	.2893136	.223457	1.295	0.200	-.1575164	.7361435
nextff	.1917858	.1980392	0.968	0.337	-.204218	.5877896
hextff	.4610618	.2306397	1.999	0.050	-.0001308	.9222544
bknow	.4140097	.2509108	1.650	0.104	-.0877174	.9157369
oknow	.358191	.2759976	1.298	0.199	-.1937004	.9100823
mobile1	.6902258	.2299894	3.001	0.004	.2303336	1.150118
_cons	-1.651583	.5904523	-2.797	0.007	-2.832265	-.4709003

Table B21: Survey Logistic Regression for Attempting to Persuade
Another's Vote in 1996 (Democrats Age 65+)

pweight: wgt   Number of obs   =   543
Strata: strata   Number of strata   =   4
PSU: psu   Number of PSUs   =   97
                                      Population size   =   532.8329
                                      F(26,   68)   =   2.18
                                      Prob > F   =   0.0056

persuad	Coef.	Std. Err.	t	P>ltl	[95% Conf. Interval]
ageold	-.3480362	.5079787	-0.685	0.495	-1.356781	.6607088
nhigh	-.3070296	.4379071	-0.701	0.485	-1.176626	.5625671
coll	-.3039978	.3533642	-0.860	0.392	-1.005709	.3977135
employ	.2088321	.3880099	0.538	0.592	-.5616785	.9793428
union	.4273323	.289204	1.478	0.143	-.1469695	1.001634
religion	.2180737	.2746775	0.794	0.429	-.3273812	.7635287
income	-.6467022	.6944355	-0.931	0.354	-2.025713	.7323089
emplos	.5456719	.2885821	1.891	0.062	-.027395	1.118739
commun	-.0114178	.0039376	-2.900	0.005	-.0192371	-.0035986
homeown	.3712978	.3039976	1.221	0.225	-.2323812	.9749768
race	.3413152	.3400505	1.004	0.318	-.3339576	1.016588
gender	-.309628	.2478565	-1.249	0.215	-.8018218	.1825658
care	-.3398962	.3847501	-0.883	0.379	-1.103934	.4241412
notv	.234175	.4201672	0.557	0.579	-.6001937	1.068544
tv	.8919643	.3168873	2.815	0.006	.2626889	1.52124
listen	.4754464	.2748701	1.730	0.087	-.0703912	1.021284
hknow	.2081127	.304658	0.683	0.496	-.3968777	.813103
lknow	-.3822347	.4490722	-0.851	0.397	-1.274003	.5095337
weak	-.5927382	.2704562	-2.192	0.031	-1.129811	-.0556658
nintff	.7433717	.3446266	2.157	0.034	.0590115	1.427732
hintff	.0094312	.3157302	0.030	0.976	-.6175463	.6364087
nextff	.1524481	.3720824	0.410	0.683	-.5864338	.89133
hextff	.0676986	.2694448	0.251	0.802	-.4673653	.6027625
bknow	.2356229	.3890267	0.606	0.546	-.5369071	1.008153
oknow	.0584147	.4874541	0.120	0.905	-.9095724	1.026402
mobile1	.568833	.2457046	2.315	0.023	.0809124	1.056754
_cons	-1.491771	.7541717	-1.978	0.051	-2.989407	.0058644

Table B22: Survey Logistic Regression for Attempting to Persuade Another's Vote in 1988 (Independents Age 65+)

pweight: wgt

Strata: strata

PSU: psu

Number of obs	=	435
Number of strata	=	4
Number of PSUs	=	47
Population size	=	812
F(25, 19)	=	3.11
Prob > F	=	0.0069

persuad	Coef.	Std. Err.	t	P>|t|	[95% Conf. Interval]	
ageold	-.3636013	.5232482	-0.695	0.491	-1.418832	.6916292
nhigh	-.107634	.5610486	-0.192	0.849	-1.239096	1.023828
coll	.2829721	.3048394	0.928	0.358	-.3317952	.8977394
employ	.0088719	.3738257	0.024	0.981	-.7450194	.7627632
union	.07764	.3246303	0.239	0.812	-.5770394	.7323194
religion	.3588662	.5657321	0.634	0.529	-.7820414	1.499774
income	.3404419	.5304015	0.642	0.524	-.7292146	1.410098
emplos	.5461158	.3221858	1.695	0.097	-.1036339	1.195865
commun	-.0072683	.0050991	-1.425	0.161	-.0175515	.0030149
homeown	.4062666	.3915784	1.038	0.305	-.3834266	1.19596
race	.5117466	.4143889	1.235	0.224	-.3239482	1.347441
gender	-.4989684	.3623141	-1.377	0.176	-1.229644	.2317077
care	.8017794	.2587182	3.099	0.003	.2800244	1.323534
notv	-.4175163	.379834	-1.099	0.278	-1.183525	.348492
tv	.6821968	.2925993	2.332	0.024	.092114	1.27228
listen	-.1942863	.3513169	-0.553	0.583	-.9027842	.5142117
hknow	.7315089	.2914356	2.510	0.016	.143773	1.319245
lknow	.2646422	.4247564	0.623	0.537	-.5919607	1.121245
nintff	.2855936	.3978453	0.718	0.477	-.516738	1.087925
hintff	.042101	.3217952	0.131	0.897	-.6068609	.6910629
nextff	.5354987	.356167	1.504	0.140	-.1827806	1.253778
hextff	.2597326	.3173897	0.818	0.418	-.3803446	.8998099
bknow	-.1014261	.4222614	-0.240	0.811	-.9529972	.7501451
oknow	.5761195	.4186454	1.376	0.176	-.2681594	1.420398
mobile1	.8602928	.2660051	3.234	0.002	.3238424	1.396743
_cons	-3.284329	.9325222	-3.522	0.001	-5.16494	-1.403719

Table B23: Survey Logistic Regression for Attempting to Persuade
Another's Vote in 1992 (Independents Age 65+)

```
pweight: wgt                    Number of obs    =        632
Strata:  strata                 Number of strata =          4
PSU:     psu                    Number of PSUs   =         64
                                Population size   =   633.7876
                                F( 25,    36)    =       1.87
                                Prob > F          =     0.0426
```

persuad	Coef.	Std. Err.	t	P>|t|	[95% Conf. Interval]
ageold	-1.107645	.4009622	-2.762	0.008	-1.909689 -.3056011
nhigh	.1091926	.3360822	0.325	0.746	-.5630719 .7814571
coll	-.0639199	.188353	-0.339	0.736	-.440682 .3128422
employ	-.0157731	.2265806	-0.070	0.945	-.4690019 .4374556
union	.0087646	.2685271	0.033	0.974	-.5283695 .5458987
religion	.10049	.2100135	0.478	0.634	-.3195995 .5205795
income	-.0535722	.5368255	-0.100	0.921	-1.127383 1.020238
emplos	.1580636	.2322923	0.680	0.499	-.3065903 .6227174
commun	-.0006966	.0024048	-0.290	0.773	-.005507 .0041138
homeown	.0572231	.2344513	0.244	0.808	-.4117493 .5261955
race	-.191542	.4439518	-0.431	0.668	-1.079578 .6964938
gender	-.2334357	.1876991	-1.244	0.218	-.6088899 .1420185
care	.5127292	.2409775	2.128	0.037	.0307025 .9947559
notv	-.3749255	.2503338	-1.498	0.139	-.8756676 .1258167
tv	.3835537	.2455662	1.562	0.124	-.1076519 .8747593
listen	.0070451	.1842678	0.038	0.970	-.3615453 .3756355
hknow	-.2056683	.2164563	-0.950	0.346	-.6386453 .2273088
lknow	-.9589123	.2704745	-3.545	0.001	-1.499942 -.4178827
nintff	.0619387	.3581081	0.173	0.863	-.6543841 .7782614
hintff	.2486731	.2515366	0.989	0.327	-.254475 .7518212
nextff	.1635475	.2302887	0.710	0.480	-.2970984 .6241935
hextff	.1467413	.2067337	0.710	0.481	-.2667876 .5602703
bknow	.3322256	.2381199	1.395	0.168	-.144085 .8085363
oknow	.5177685	.2616245	1.979	0.052	-.0055583 1.041095
mobile1	.0789083	.2313139	0.341	0.734	-.3837884 .5416051
_cons	-1.071755	.4229385	-2.534	0.014	-1.917758 -.2257522

Table B24: Survey Logistic Regression for Attempting to Persuade Another's Vote in 1996 (Independents Age 65+)

pweight:	wgt		Number of obs	=	353
Strata:	strata		Number of strata	=	4
PSU:	psu		Number of PSUs	=	85
			Population size	=	381.7859
			F(25, 57)	=	2.25
			Prob > F	=	0.0059

persuad	Coef.	Std. Err.	t	P>|t|	[95% Conf. Interval]	
ageold	-.4174634	.5003917	-0.834	0.407	-1.413086	.5781592
nhigh	.3281463	.6558848	0.500	0.618	-.9768586	1.633151
coll	-.071217	.3751387	-0.190	0.850	-.8176253	.6751914
employ	-.7380917	.3083886	-2.393	0.019	-1.351688	-.1244951
union	.0195281	.389709	0.050	0.960	-.7558705	.7949266
religion	.3128337	.2956747	1.058	0.293	-.2754662	.9011337
income	.6175899	.6866667	0.899	0.371	-.7486614	1.983841
emplos	.2333233	.2939687	0.794	0.430	-.3515821	.8182287
commun	-.0052425	.0044858	-1.169	0.246	-.0141678	.0036827
homeown	-.0421084	.3535068	-0.119	0.905	-.7454761	.6612593
race	-.7703792	.6511613	-1.183	0.240	-2.065986	.5252275
gender	-.3418673	.3287435	-1.040	0.301	-.9959638	.3122292
care	1.424999	.4222271	3.375	0.001	.5848998	2.265099
notv	.420465	.4082555	1.030	0.306	-.3918354	1.232765
tv	.6397893	.4046733	1.581	0.118	-.1653837	1.444962
listen	.8035458	.3385171	2.374	0.020	.1300029	1.477089
hknow	.3135077	.3289525	0.953	0.343	-.3410045	.9680198
lknow	-.4884486	.5457558	-0.895	0.373	-1.574331	.5974341
nintff	-.2106843	.4739492	-0.445	0.658	-1.153695	.7323259
hintff	-.0050866	.366163	-0.014	0.989	-.733636	.7234629
nextff	-.2855209	.3714926	-0.769	0.444	-1.024675	.4536328
hextff	-.9954716	.438264	-2.271	0.026	-1.867479	-.1234638
bknow	.1148915	.4120303	0.279	0.781	-.7049196	.9347026
oknow	.6810346	.4126217	1.651	0.103	-.1399531	1.502022
mobile1	.3320111	.2699089	1.230	0.222	-.2050229	.869045
_cons	-2.674025	.8170592	-3.273	0.002	-4.299716	-1.048333

Table B25: Survey Logistic Regression for Being Contacted by a
Political Party in 1988 (Age 65+)

pweight: wgt			Number of obs	=	1442
Strata: strata			Number of strata	=	4
PSU: psu			Number of PSUs	=	47
			Population size	=	2638
			F(13, 31)	=	8.04
			Prob > F	=	0.0000

mobile1	Coef.	Std. Err.	t	P>|t|	[95% Conf. Interval]	
ageold	.7282201	.2290375	3.179	0.003	.266322	1.190118
income	.6816321	.2663483	2.559	0.014	.1444895	1.218775
nhigh	.0002255	.2164381	0.001	0.999	-.4362635	.4367145
coll	.2499279	.1756374	1.423	0.162	-.1042787	.6041344
weak	-.2247691	.1480755	-1.518	0.136	-.5233918	.0738535
ind	-.0573032	.2011167	-0.285	0.777	-.4628938	.3482873
commun	-.0047166	.0027978	-1.68	0.099	-.0103589	.0009257
religion	.2900227	.2015392	1.439	0.157	-.1164198	.6964653
homeown	.6277573	.1909446	3.288	0.002	.2426808	1.012834
employ	-.2016134	.1788551	-1.127	0.266	-.5623091	.1590823
race	.2240947	.2201124	1.018	0.314	-.2198042	.6679937
gender	.0610051	.1416331	0.431	0.669	-.2246253	.3466355
care	.5095869	.1938837	2.628	0.012	.1185832	.9005905
_cons	-2.441719	.3625215	-6.735	0.000	-3.172813	-1.710624

Table B26: Survey Logistic Regression for Being Contacted by a
Political Party in 1992 (Age 65+)

pweight: wgt			Number of obs	=	1887
Strata: strata			Number of strata	=	4
PSU: psu			Number of PSUs	=	65
			Population size	=	1894.9676
			F(13, 49)	=	5.55
			Prob > F	=	0.0000

mobile1	Coef.	Std. Err.	t	P>|t|	[95% Conf. Interval]	
ageold	.2121368	.2007865	1.057	0.295	-.1893606	.6136342
income	.8187095	.2536027	3.228	0.002	.3115996	1.325819
nhigh	-.3214017	.2430565	-1.322	0.191	-.8074233	.1646199
coll	.2093903	.1238553	1.691	0.096	-.0382737	.4570544
weak	-.2795514	.1249406	-2.237	0.029	-.5293856	-.0297172
ind	-.4530969	.1299242	-3.487	0.001	-.7128963	-.1932974
commun	.0006428	.0019223	0.334	0.739	-.0032011	.0044866
religion	.1680041	.1391862	1.207	0.232	-.1103158	.4463241
homeown	.4679079	.1431571	3.268	0.002	.1816476	.7541682
employ	-.1879459	.154054	-1.220	0.227	-.4959958	.1201041
race	.0288163	.229523	0.126	0.901	-.4301433	.4877758
gender	-.1559675	.0993341	-1.570	0.122	-.3545983	.0426633
care	.3779575	.169212	2.234	0.029	.0395972	.7163178
_cons	-2.167964	.275566	-7.867	0.000	-2.718992	-1.616936

Table B27: Survey Logistic Regression for Being Contacted by a
Political Party in 1996 (Age 65+)

pweight:	wgt		Number of obs	=	1376
Strata:	strata		Number of strata	=	4
PSU:	psu		Number of PSUs	=	116
			Population size	=	1377.643
			F(13, 100)	=	4.81
			Prob > F	=	0.0000

mobile1	Coef.	Std. Err.	t	P>|t|	[95% Conf. Interval]	
ageold	.6401234	.2082371	3.074	0.003	.2275283	1.052719
income	.4005112	.2957046	1.354	0.178	-.1853895	.9864119
nhigh	.0089084	.2497372	0.036	0.972	-.4859137	.5037306
coll	.6923719	.1630604	4.246	0.000	.3692888	1.015455
weak	-.1368658	.1893797	-0.723	0.471	-.5120973	.2383657
ind	-.2419576	.1812796	-1.335	0.185	-.60114	.1172247
commun	.0016836	.0021698	0.776	0.439	-.0026156	.0059827
religion	.1106875	.1531168	0.723	0.471	-.1926937	.4140687
homeown	.7227138	.1815067	3.982	0.000	.3630815	1.082346
employ	-.0417713	.1920718	-0.217	0.828	-.422337	.3387944
race	-.3347006	.2233856	-1.498	0.137	-.7773104	.1079092
gender	.0756523	.1535428	0.493	0.623	-.2285731	.3798778
care	.4225898	.1808673	2.336	0.021	.0642243	.7809552
_cons	-2.577602	.395793	-6.512	0.000	-3.361815	-1.793388

Table B28: Survey Logistic Regression for Being Contacted by a Political Party in 1988 (Democrats Age 65+)

pweight: wgt			Number of obs	=	519	
Strata: strata			Number of strata	=	4	
PSU: psu			Number of PSUs	=	47	
			Population size	=	955	
			F(12, 32)	=	6.36	
			Prob > F	=	0.0000	

mobile1	Coef.	Std. Err.	t	P>|t|	[95% Conf. Interval]	
ageold	.8497944	.2981964	2.850	0.007	.248424	1.451165
income	1.12783	.5197546	2.170	0.036	.0796453	2.176015
nhigh	.4807757	.3598935	1.336	0.189	-.2450186	1.20657
coll	.3617349	.2627562	1.377	0.17	-.1681636	.8916333
weak	-.2355233	.1943281	-1.212	0.232	-.6274232	.1563767
commun	-.0019609	.0041233	-0.476	0.637	-.0102764	.0063547
religion	.8545071	.330693	2.584	0.013	.1876011	1.521413
homeown	.7478401	.2546241	2.937	0.005	.2343417	1.261339
employ	-.3203482	.2659669	-1.204	0.235	-.8567215	.2160251
race	.3961322	.2665444	1.486	0.145	-.1414058	.9336702
gender	-.0150111	.3028608	-0.050	0.961	-.6257882	.5957659
care	.5287411	.3173523	1.666	0.103	-.1112608	1.168743
_cons	-3.401572	.5777124	-5.888	0.000	-4.56664	-2.236504

Table B29: Survey Logistic Regression for Being Contacted by a
Political Party in 1992 (Democrats Age 65+)

```
pweight: wgt                    Number of obs    =      663
Strata:  strata                 Number of strata =        4
PSU:     psu                    Number of PSUs   =       65
                                Population size   = 666.8248
                                F( 12,    50)    =     2.17
                                Prob > F          =   0.0282
```

mobile1	Coef.	Std. Err.	t	P>|t|	[95% Conf. Interval]	
ageold	.1815633	.2751185	0.660	0.512	-.3685701	.7316967
income	.7552674	.4782301	1.579	0.119	-.2010127	1.711548
nhigh	-.3185065	.2676871	-1.190	0.239	-.85378	.216767
coll	.4802194	.2494503	1.925	0.059	-.0185874	.9790262
weak	-.4201559	.1961067	-2.142	0.036	-.8122955	-.0280163
commun	.0030927	.0032187	0.961	0.340	-.0033436	.009529
religion	-.0600419	.205104	-0.293	0.771	-.4701727	.3500888
homeown	.3832273	.2180241	1.758	0.084	-.0527388	.8191934
employ	-.1279251	.2319064	-0.552	0.583	-.5916506	.3358005
race	-.0875223	.262405	-0.334	0.740	-.6122335	.4371889
gender	-.1148286	.2084368	-0.551	0.584	-.5316238	.3019666
care	.3862038	.2962743	1.304	0.197	-.2062333	.9786409
_cons	-2.087992	.4385546	-4.761	0.000	-2.964936	-1.211048

Table B30: Survey Logistic Regression for Being Contacted by a Political Party in 1996 (Democrats Age 65+)

pweight:	wgt			Number of obs	=	548
Strata:	strata			Number of strata	=	4
PSU:	psu			Number of PSUs	=	98
				Population size	=	536.5438
				F(12, 83)	=	2.87
				Prob > F	=	0.0024

mobile1	Coef.	Std. Err.	t	P>|t|	[95% Conf.	Interval]
ageold	1.138641	.3589767	3.172	0.002	.4258845	1.851398
income	.6802301	.4863906	1.399	0.165	-.2855098	1.64597
nhigh	.1801197	.4001781	0.450	0.654	-.6144434	.9746827
coll	.7365634	.2543461	2.896	0.005	.2315534	1.241573
weak	.0132149	.2228908	0.059	0.953	-.42934	.4557698
commun	.0031489	.0039409	0.799	0.426	-.0046758	.0109736
religion	-.0773202	.2176737	-0.355	0.723	-.5095165	.3548761
homeown	.3760601	.2592327	1.451	0.150	-.1386525	.8907727
employ	.5134696	.2654256	1.935	0.056	-.0135391	1.040478
race	-.3350049	.2690941	-1.245	0.216	-.8692975	.1992878
gender	.1441643	.2285141	0.631	0.530	-.3095558	.5978844
care	.3446455	.3068159	1.123	0.264	-.2645447	.9538358
_cons	-2.998479	.6790486	-4.416	0.000	-4.346746	-1.650212

Table B31: Survey Logistic Regression for Being Contacted by a
Political Party in 1988 (Independents Age 65+)

pweight: wgt				Number of obs	=	435
Strata: strata				Number of strata	=	4
PSU: psu				Number of PSUs	=	47
				Population size	=	812
				F(12, 83)	=	3.22
				Prob > F	=	0.0046

mobile1	Coef.	Std. Err.	t	P>|t|	[95% Conf. Interval]	
ageold	.565191	.402504	1.404	0.167	-.2465356	1.376918
income	.5498475	.7411859	0.742	0.462	-.9448963	2.044591
nhigh	-.515967	.425556	-1.212	0.232	-1.374182	.3422484
coll	.3595841	.3236158	1.111	0.273	-.2930494	1.012218
commun	-.0151174	.0045547	-3.319	0.002	-.0243029	-.005932
religion	-.0259316	.4793689	-0.054	0.957	-.9926711	.9408079
homeown	.7690937	.3994856	1.925	0.061	-.0365458	1.574733
employ	-.1624198	.304614	-0.533	0.597	-.7767324	.4518928
race	-.0718731	.5298747	-0.136	0.893	-1.140467	.9967211
gender	.3047875	.2793905	1.091	0.281	-.258657	.8682321
care	.7324201	.2847946	2.572	0.014	.1580769	1.306763
_cons	-2.138039	.6421189	-3.330	0.002	-3.432995	-.8430828

Table B32: Survey Logistic Regression for Being Contacted by a
Political Party in 1988 (Independents Age 65+)

pweight: wgt				Number of obs	=	636
Strata: strata				Number of strata	=	4
PSU: psu				Number of PSUs	=	64
				Population size	=	637.2726
				F(11, 50)	=	3.07
				Prob > F	=	0.0033

mobile1	Coef.	Std. Err.	t	P>|t|	[95% Conf. Interval]	
ageold	.4276771	.3734506	1.145	0.257	-.3193354	1.174689
income	1.257635	.450672	2.791	0.007	.3561569	2.159113
nhigh	-.1226976	.3774705	-0.325	0.746	-.877751	.6323558
coll	.0514496	.2258486	0.228	0.821	-.4003149	.5032141
commun	-.003395	.0041598	-0.816	0.418	-.0117157	.0049257
religion	.0961473	.2542824	0.378	0.707	-.4124932	.6047879
homeown	.4227223	.2438518	1.734	0.088	-.0650539	.9104984
employ	-.1808783	.2654456	-0.681	0.498	-.7118486	.350092
race	.5678277	.4305083	1.319	0.192	-.2933171	1.428972
gender	-.2862477	.1997762	-1.433	0.157	-.6858596	.1133642
care	.3945301	.2434211	1.621	0.110	-.0923845	.8814448
_cons	-2.64349	.4383036	-6.031	0.000	-3.520228	-1.766753

Table B33: Survey Logistic Regression for Being Contacted by a
Political Party in 1996 (Independents Age 65+)

pweight: wgt   Number of obs   =   354
Strata: strata   Number of strata   =   4
PSU: psu   Number of PSUs   =   86
                                Population size   = 382.4818
                                F(11,   72)   =   4.20
                                Prob > F   =   0.0001

mobile1	Coef.	Std. Err.	t	P>|t|	[95% Conf. Interval]	
ageold	1.006304	.4358894	2.309	0.023	.1391814	1.873427
income	.2152583	.6031047	0.357	0.722	-.9845089	1.415026
nhigh	-.4272434	.4868066	-0.878	0.383	-1.395657	.54117
coll	.7147492	.3255514	2.196	0.031	.0671237	1.362375
commun	.0015606	.0051846	0.301	0.764	-.0087531	.0118744
religion	-.2560286	.3003625	-0.852	0.396	-.8535453	.3414881
homeown	1.183989	.3237101	3.658	0.000	.5400268	1.827952
employ	-.2329297	.3449632	-0.675	0.501	-.9191714	.453312
race	.2109164	.4725736	0.446	0.657	-.729183	1.151016
gender	.0221908	.3466825	0.064	0.949	-.6674712	.7118528
care	.1153833	.330428	0.349	0.728	-.5419432	.7727097
_cons	-2.4565	.6908824	-3.556	0.001	-3.830885	-1.082115

Bibliography

"Proposed Medicare Reforms." ABC, 7 May 1995, *World News Sunday.*

"Senate Republicans Present Plan to Balance Budget: Plan Calls for Elimination of 140 Agencies, Changes in Medicaid, Medicare." CBS, 9 May 1995, *Evening News.*

Alvarez, Michael and Charles Franklin. "Uncertainty and Political Perceptions." *Journal of Politics* 56 (1994): 671-88.

Ansolabehere, Stephen, Roy Behr, and Shanto Iyengar. *The Media Game: American Politics in the Television Age.* New York: Macmillan Publishing Company, 1993.

Bartels, Larry. "Uninformed Votes: Information Effects in Presidential Elections." *American Journal of Political Science* 40, no. 1 (1996): 194-230.

Belli, Robert, Santa Traugott, and Steven J. Rosenstone. "Reducing Over-Reporting of Voter Turnout: An Experiment using Source Monitoring Framework." *Technical Report Number 35.* Available at: http://www.umich.edu/~nes/resources/techrpts/tech-abs/tech-ab35.htm. Accessed June 17, 1997.

Binstock, Robert. "Older Voters and the 1992 Presidential Election". *The Gerontologist.* 32 (1992): 601-606.

Blendon, Robert, Drew Altman, John Benson, Humphrey Taylor, Matt James, and Mark Smith. "The Implications of the 1992 Presidential Election for Health Care Reform." *Journal of the American Medical Association.* 268, no. 23 (1992): 3371-3376.

Blendon, Robert, Drew Altman, John Benson, Matt James, Diane Rowland, Patrician Neuman, Robert Lietman, and Tracey Hymans.

"The Public's Views of the Future of Medicare." *Journal of the American Medical Association.* 274, no. 20 (1995): 1645-1648.

Blendon, Robert, John Benson, Mollyann Brodie, Drew Altman, Diane Rowland, Patricia Neuman, and Matt James. "Voters and Health Care in the 1996 Election (Public Opinion and Health Care)." *Journal of the American Medical Association.* 277, no. 15 (1997): 1253-1259.

Brady, Henry and Sniderman, Paul. "Attitude Attribution: A Group Basis for Political Reasoning." *American Political Science Review.* 79 (1985): 1061-78.

Braungart, Richard, and Margaret Braungart. "Life-Course and Generational Politics." *Annual Review of Sociology.* 12 (1986): 205-236.

Brodie, Mollyann, Lee Ann Brady, and Drew Altman. "Media Coverage of Managed Care: Is There a Negative Bias." *Health Affairs* 17 (January/February 1998): 9-25.

Brodie, Mollyann. "Political Institutions, Participation, and Media Evaluations: Influences on Health Care Policy." Ph.D. diss., Harvard University., 1995.

Congressional Quarterly Almanac: 104th Congress, 1st Session...1995, Volume LI. Washington, D.C.: Congressioal Quarterly,1995.

Conover, Pamela and Stanley Feldman. "Candidate Perceptions in an Ambigious World: Campaigns, Cues and Inference Processes." *American Journal of Political Science* 33 (1989): 912-40.

Conover, Pamela and Stanley Feldman. "The Origins and Meaning of Liberal/Conservative Self-Identification." *American Journal of Political Science.* 25 (1981): 617-645.

Converse, Philip. "The Nature of Belief Systems in Mass Publics." In *Ideology and Discontent,* ed. David Apter. New York: The Free Press, 1964.

Corrado, Anthony. "Financing the 1996 Election." In *The Election of 1996: Reports and Interpretations.* Chatham, NJ: Chatham House Publishers, 1995.

Crenshaw, Albert. "Look Before Leaping Into 'Managed' Medicare." *The Washington Post,* 30 April 1995, Financial section, final edition.

Dalton, Russell, Paul Beck, and Robert Huckfeldt. "Partisan Cues and the Media: Information Flows in the 1992 Presidential Election." *American Political Science Review* 92 (March 1998): 111-126.

Delli Carpini, Michael. and Scott Keeter. *What Americans Know about Politics and Why It Matters.* New Haven, CT: Yale University Press, 1996.

Dodge, Robert. "Two Key Panels Back GOP on Medicare: House Committees' Votes Divide Along Party Lines." *The Dallas Morning News,* 12 October 1995, News section, home final edition.

Facts about Newspapers 1996. Washington, D.C.: American Newspaper Publishers Association, 1996.

Fan, David and Lois Norem. "The Media and the Fate of the Medicare Catastrophic Extension Act." *Journal of Health Policy Politics and Law* 92 (Spring 1992): 39-70.

Fiorina, Morris. *Retrospective Voting in American National Elections.* New Haven: Yale University Press, 1981.

Furnham, Adrian. "Relationship Between Knowledge of and Attitudes Towards AIDS." *Psychological Reports* 71 no. 3:1-2 (1992): 1149-1151.

Graber, Doris. *Processing the News: How People Tame the Information Tide,* 2nd ed. New York: Longman, 1988.

Hastie, Reid and Bernadette Park. "The Relationship between Memory and Judgement Depends on Whether the Judgement Task is Memory-Based or On-Line." *Psychological Review* 93(3): 258+.

Himelfarb, Richard. *Catastrophic Politics: The Rise and Fall of the Medicare Catastrophic Coverage Act of 1988.* University Park, PA: Pennsylvania State University Press, 1995.

Hudson, Robert and John Strate. "Aging and Political Systems." In *Handbook of Aging and the Social Sciences,* eds. Robert Binstock and Ethel Shanas. New York: Van Nostrand Reinhold, 1985.

Hudson, Robert. "Tomorrow's Able Elders: Implications for the State." *The Gerontologist.* 27 (1987): 405-409.

Imperato, Alison M. "Acquired Immunodeficiency Syndrome and Suburban Adolescents: Knowledge, Attitudes, Behaviors, and Risks. *Journal of Community Health* 21, no.5 (1996), 329-348.

Iyengar, Shanto and Donald Kinder. *News That Matters.* Chicago: University of Chicago Press, 1987.

Iyengar, Shanto. *Is Anyone Responsible? How Television Frames Political Issues.* Chicago: University of Chicago Press, 1991.

Jamieson, Kathleen Hall and Karyln Kohrs Campbell. *The Interplay of Influence: Mass Media and Their Publics in News, Advertising, and Politics,* 3rd ed. Belmont: Wadsworth, 1992.

Johnson, Haynes and David Broder. *The System: The American Way of Politics at the Breaking Point*. Boston: Little, Brown and Company, 1996.

Kingdon, John. *Agendas, Alternatives and Public Policies*. New York: HarperCollins Publishers, 1995.

Kingdon, John. *Congressmen's Voting Decisions*. New York: Harper and Row, 1981.

Krosnick, Jon and Donald Kinder. "Altering the Foundations of Support for the President Through Priming." *American Political Science Review*. 84, no. 2 (1990): 497-512.

Krosnick, Jon and Laura Brannon. "The Impact of the Gulf War on the Ingredients of Presidential Evaluations: Multidimensional Effects of Political Involvement." *American Political Science Review*. 87 (1993): 963-975.

Lammers, William. *Public Policy and the Aging*. Washington, D.C.: Congressional Quarterly Press, 1983.

Lazarsfeld, Paul, Bernard Berelson, and Hazel Gaudet. *The People's Choice: How the Voter Makes up His Mind in a Presidential Campaign*. New York: Duell, Sloan and Pearce, 1944.

Leighley, Jan and Jonathan Nagler. "Individual and Systematic Influences on Turnout: Who Votes?" *Journal of Politics*. 54 (1992): 718-740.

Lodge, Milton and Kathleen McGraw. "Introduction." In *Political Judgment: Structure and Process*, eds. Milton Lodge and Kathleen McGraw. Ann Arbor: The University of Michigan Press, 1996.

Lodge, Milton, Kathleen McGraw, and Patrick Stroh. "An Impression-Driven Model of Candidate Evaluation." *American Political Science Review* 83 (1989): 399-419.

Lodge, Milton, Marco Steenbergen, and Shawn Brau. "The Responsive Voter: Campaign Information and the Dynamics of Candidate Evaluation." *American Political Science Review* 89 no. 2 (1995): 309-326.

Lupia, Arthur. "Short Cuts Versus Encyclopedias: Information and Voting Behavior in California Insurance Reform Elections." *American Political Science Review* 88 (1994): 63-76.

Luskin, Robert. "Measuring Political Sophistication." *American Journal of Political Science* 31 (1987): 856-899.

McGraw, Kathleen and Neil Pinney. 'The Effects of General and Domain Specific Expertise on Political Memory and Judgment." *Social Cognition* 8 (1990: 9-30.

"A Medicare Dilemma: More 65 Year-Olds." *The Washington Post*, 25 April 1995, Health section, final edition.

"Medicare Cuts Vetoed as Part of Budget Reconciliation." In *Congressional Quarterly Almanac: 104th Congress, 1st Session...1995, Volume LI.* Washington, D.C.: Congressional Quarterly, 1995.

Miller, Warren E., and the National Election Studies. *American National Election Study, 1988: Pre- and Post-Election Survey* [computer file]. Ann Arbor, MI: Center for Political Studies, University of Michigan, 1989 (original producer). 2nd ICPSR ed. Ann Arbor, MI: Inter-University Consortium for Political and Social Research, 1989 (producer and distributor).

Miller, Warren E., Donald R. Kinder, Steven J. Rosenstone, and the National Election Studies. *American National Election Study, 1992: Pre- and Post-Election Surveys [Enhanced with 1990 and 1991 Data]* [Computer File]. Conducted by University of Michigan, Center for Political Studies. ICPSR ed. Ann Arbor, MI: University of Michigan Center for Political Studies, and Inter-University Consortium for Political and Social Research [producers], 1993. Ann Arbor, MI: Inter-University Consortium for Political and Social Research [distributor], 1993.

Monroe, Alan. "Public Opinion and Public Policy, 1980-1993." *Public Opinion Quarterly* 62 (Spring 1998): 6-28.

Moon, Marilyn. *Medicare Now and in the Future.* Aldershot: Ashgate, 1997.

Neuman, Russell. *The Paradox of Mass Politics: Knowledge and Opinion in the American Electorate.* Cambridge, MA: Harvard University Press, 1986.

Nicholas, Lionel, Neil Orr, and Priscilla Daniels. "Reliability of a Knowledge of AIDS Scale: A Replication." *Psychological Reports* 79, no. 2 (1996): 59-60.

Nie, Norman, Sidney Verba, and John Petrocik, *The Changing American Voter.* Cambridge, MA: Harvard University Press, 1976.

Page, Benjamin and Robert Shapiro. *The Rational Public.* Chicago: University of Chicago Press, 1992.

Page, Benjamin, Robert Shapiro, and Glenn Dempsey. "What Moves Public Opinion?" *American Political Science Review* 81(March 1987): 175-190.

Page, Benjamin, Robert Shapiro, and Glenn Dempset. "What Moves Public Opinion." *American Political Science Review* 81 (March 1987): 23-44.

Peterson, Steven and Albert Somit. *The Political Behavior of Older Americans.* New York: Garland Publishing, Inc., 1994.

Pew Center for the People and the Press. April 1996 Media Consumption
   Survey. Available at: http://www.people-press.org/mediaque.htm.
   Accessed July 22, 1998.

"Proposed Medicare Reforms." ABC, 7 May 1995, *World News Sunday.*

Primer on the Federal Budget. Menlo Park: The Henry J. Kaiser Family
   Foundation, 1995.

Reeves, Keith. *Voting Hopes or Fears?: White Voters, Black Candidates &*
   Racial Politics in America. New York: Oxford University Press, 1997.

Rhodebeck, Laurie. 1993. "The Politics of Greed? Political Preferences
   Among the Elderly." *Journal of Politics* 55, no. 2 (1993): 342-364.

Robertson, David. "Surrogates for Party Identification in the Rational
   Choice Framework." In *Party Identification and Beyond:*
   Representations of Voting and Party Competition, eds. Ian Budge,
   Ivor Crewe, and Dennis Farlie. London: Wiley, 1976.

Rogers, Everett and James Dearing. "Agenda-Setting Research: Where
   Has It Been, Where Is It Going?" In *Communication Yearbook 11,*
   ed. J.A. Anderson. Beverly Hills: Sage Publications, 1988.

Rosenstone, Steven and John Hansen. *Mobilization, Participation, and*
   Democracy in America. New York: Macmillan Publishing Company,
   1993.

Rosenstone, Steven, Donald Kinder, Warren Miller and the National
   Election Studies. *American National Election Study, 1996: Pre- and*
   Post-Election Surveys [Computer file accessed from the website].
   Conducted by University of Michigan, Center for Political Studies.
   ICPSR ed. Ann Arbor, MI: University of Michigan Center for
   Political Studies, and Inter-University Consortium for Political and
   Social Research [producers], 1997.

"Senate Republicans Present Plan to Balance Budget: Plan Calls for
   Elimination of 140 Agencies, Changes in Medicaid, Medicare." CBS,
   9 May 1995, *Evening News.*

Smith, Eric. The Unchanging American Voter. Berkeley: University of
   California Press, 1989.

Sniderman, Paul, Richard Brody, and Philip Tetlock. *Reasoning and*
   Choice: Explorations in Political Psychology. New York: Cambridge
   University Press, 1991.

Snow, Tony. "Medicare's Going Broke – and Fast!" *USA Today,* 1 May
   1995, News section, final edition.

Stanley, H.W. "The Parties, the President, and the 1994 Midterm
   Elections." in *The Clinton Presidency: First Appraisals,* eds. Colin

Campbell and Bert Rockman. New Jersey: Chatham House Publishers, 1996.

Statistical Abstract of the United States: 1996, 116th ed. Washington, D.C.: U.S. Government Printing Office, 1996.

Stimson, James. *Public Opinion in America: Moods, Cycles, and Swings.* Boulder, CO: Westview Press, 1991.

Sullivan, John, James Piereson, and George Marcus. "Ideological Constraint in the Mass Public: A Methodological Critique and Some News Findings." *American Journal of Political Science* 23 (1978): 233-249.

VanLandingham, Mark, Nancy Grandjean, Somboon Suprasert, Werasit Sittitrai. "Dimensions of AIDS Knowledge and Risky Sexual Practices: A Study of Northern Thai Males." *Archives of Sexual Behavior* 26, no. (3) (1997): 269-294.

Verba, Sidney, and Norman Nie. *Participation in America: Political Democracy and Social Equality.* New York: Harper & Row, 1972.

Verba, Sidney, Kay Schlozman, and Henry Brady. *Voice and Equality: Civic Voluntarism in American Politics.* Cambridge, MA: Harvard University Press, 1995.

Weisskopf, Michael and David Maraniss. "Gingrich's War of Words: How He and His Legions Marshaled the Forces of Rhetoric to Change Medicare." *Washington Post National Weekly.* 6-12 November 1995, national weekly edition.

West, Darryl. *Air Wars: Television Advertising in Election Campaigns 1952-1996*, 2nd ed. Washington, D.C.: Congressional Quarterly Inc., 1997.

Wolfinger, Raymond and Steven Rosenstone. *Who Votes?* New Haven: Yale University Press, 1980.

Zagumny, Matthew, and Rick Deckbar. "Willingness to Work with and Sympathy for HIV-Positive Coworkers: An Experimental Examination of Mode Transmission, Concern, and Knowledge." *Psychological Reports* 77, no. (2) (1995): 571-577.

Zaller, John. "The Myth of Massive Media Impact Revived: New Support for a Discredited Idea." In *Political Persuasion and Attitude Change* eds. Diana Mutz, Paul Sniderman, and Richard Brody. Ann Arbor: The University of Michigan Press, 1996.

Zaller, John. *The Nature and Origins of Mass Opinion.* New York: Cambridge University Press, 1992.

Index